get quilting

with Angela & Cloe

14 Projects for Kids to Sew

Angela Walters and Cloe Walters

stashBOOKS®
an imprint of C&T Publishing

Text copyright © 2015 by Angela Walters

Photography and artwork copyright © 2015 by C&T Publishing, Inc.

Publisher: Amy Marson

Creative Director: Gailen Runge

Art Director: Kristy Zacharias

Editor: Liz Aneloski

Technical Editors: Sadhana Wray and Gailen Runge

Cover/Book Designer: April Mostek

Production Coordinator: Rue Flaherty

Production Editor: Alice Mace Nakanishi

Illustrator: Jenny Davis

Photo Assistant: Mary Peyton Peppo

Photo Stylist: Lauren Toker

Cover photography by Briana Gray, style photography by Nissa Brehmer, and instructional photography by Diane Pedersen, unless otherwise noted

Published by Stash Books, an imprint of C&T Publishing, Inc., P.O. Box 1456, Lafayette, CA 94549

Library of Congress Cataloging-in-Publication Data

Walters, Angela, 1979-

Get quilting with Angela & Cloe : 14 projects for kids to sew / Angela Walters and Cloe Walters.

   pages cm

Audience: Age 8-14.

ISBN 978-1-60705-955-4 (softcover)

1. Quilting. 2. Handicraft for children. I. Walters, Cloe, 2005- II. Title. III. Title: Get quilting with Angela and Cloe.

TT835.W356544 2015

746.46--dc23

                2014031104

Printed in China

10 9 8 7 6 5 4 3 2 1

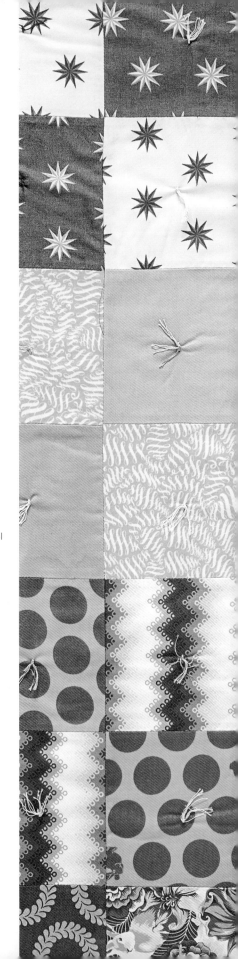

dedication

For Carl Ford, the best grandpa and great-grandpa ever.

acknowledgments

A huge thank-you to the people who made this book possible. Cloe and I have had a lot of help. Huge thanks to Kristi for binding, Ruth for keeping everything organized, and the pile of Post-it Notes that gave their lives so this book could exist.

Also, a special thank-you to the people at C&T Publishing, who trusted my vision and invested in me.

Photo by Briana Gray

contents

introduction

Photo by Briana Gray

FROM ANGELA:

It has been said that those who sleep under a quilt sleep under a blanket of love. Cloe and I couldn't agree more! It is so awesome to create an item that will warm and comfort others. The art of making quilts has been around for centuries, and we want to make sure it continues throughout the centuries to come. We hope this book will play a small part in making that happen. My name is Angela Walters, and I love making quilts. I didn't learn how to quilt until I was in my twenties. Although I got a relatively late start, I am so glad I learned. If you don't know how to make quilts yet, I hope you will join us on this journey as we show you how to make quilts and quilted projects from start to finish. Happy quilting!

FROM CLOE:

My mom started her machine-quilting business before I was even born. I have been around quilts my whole life. I have always loved to look at them and have wanted to know how to make them. One day, I asked my mom to show me how to sew. She showed me a few things and then told me to have fun. I would sew while she worked on her quilting machine. I love making quilts and projects. And I really love giving them to family members and friends. I had so much fun working on this book. I think my favorite part was picking out the fabrics. Thanks for reading!

getting started

Have you wanted to learn how to make a quilt but you weren't sure where to start? If so, this book is for you. Cloe and I love making quilts, and we can't wait to show you how to make your own quilts and quilted projects from start to finish.

about the book

We have organized the book into four sections. In the first and second sections, we walk you through each step of the quiltmaking process, from choosing fabric to sewing, quilting, and finishing. The third section has three simple projects (pot holders, place mats, and a quilted water bottle holder) to get you started and help you learn and practice new skills. The fourth section has a bunch of different projects you can make using your new quilting skills—in order of skill level: a pillow, a rug, a bed runner, a school supply roll, and seven awesome quilts. These projects all follow the same basic process as making a quilt but are slightly adapted depending on the quilted project.

what is a quilt?

Before you can make a quilt, you need to know what it is. A quilt is a blanket made of three layers held together with stitching. People usually think of quilts as being used on beds, but they can also be wall art, or the quilting techniques can be used to make other useful, decorative objects. The top layer is called the *quilt top* and is usually sewn together as a patchwork, but it can also be a single fabric. The bottom layer is the back of the quilt and is also a piece of fabric. It can be a single fabric or pieced from several fabrics. The middle layer of a quilt is the batting. It makes the quilt warm and cuddly.

supplies

Before you get started, you should have the right tools. In this section, Cloe and I will tell you all about the supplies needed to start your quilting journey.

note _____

All the supplies can be found at local quilt shops, fabric stores, large craft stores, or online.

NOTIONS

Some basic supplies you will need include straight pins and a pincushion, scissors, all-purpose sewing thread, an iron, and an ironing board.

SEWING MACHINE

To make the projects in this book, you will need a sewing machine. You may already have a sewing machine you can use. But if you need to buy one, don't worry about getting one with all the extra features. All you need is a sewing machine that can sew a good straight stitch, and a ¼" presser foot. A walking foot is helpful as well.

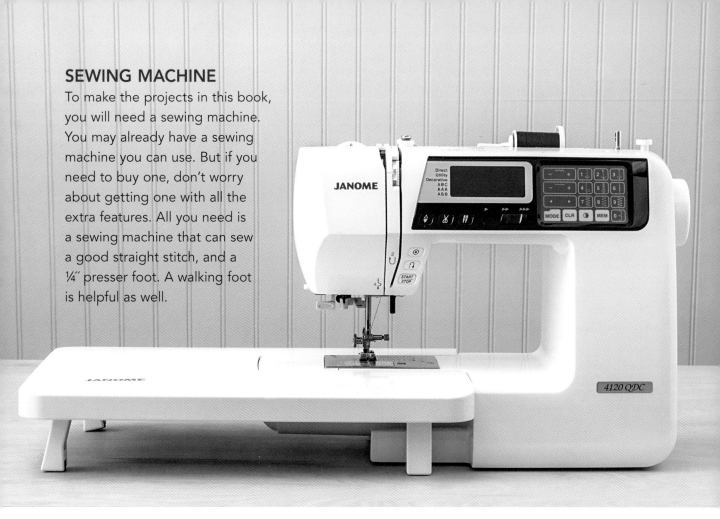

ROTARY CUTTER, RULER, AND CUTTING MAT

I am so glad I wasn't a quilter in the 1800s! Back then, quilters had to use scissors to cut each piece separately. Now we have a much faster and more accurate method: cutting with the rotary cutter, ruler, and cutting mat.

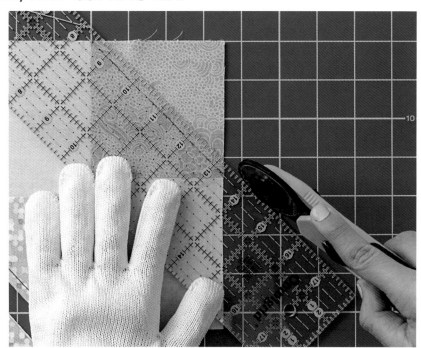

A rotary cutter is a cutting tool with a handle and a circular blade. It makes cutting fabric much quicker. There are several brands and types of rotary cutters, but they all have a safety mechanism to keep the blade covered when not in use.

You should also get a safety glove to help prevent getting cut by the rotary cutter's sharp blade.

note _____

You will learn how to use the rotary cutter in Cutting (page 18).

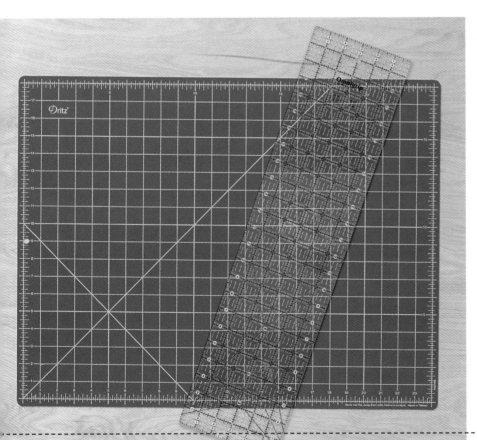

To use the rotary cutter, you will also need a ruler and cutting mat.

A long acrylic ruler designed for use with a rotary cutter helps you make straight cuts and acts as a guide for the rotary cutter. When you use a rotary cutter, the cutting mat will be the surface for cutting the fabric. The mat protects your table from getting sliced with the rotary cutter. It has lines on it to help line up the fabric and the ruler. I think the 6″ × 24″ ruler is the most versatile.

FABRIC

The best part about quilting is picking out the fabric. At least that's what Cloe and I think. There are so many colors, patterns, and types of fabric; it makes it so easy to make your quilt just how you imagine it. There are so many options available that it can be hard to know what sort of fabric you should pick. Let's talk about the kinds of fabrics we used in this book.

QUILTER'S COTTON

Cotton is the most popular fabric choice for making quilts. Although the fabric is soft, the weave is firm, which makes sewing a lot easier. It can also handle being used and washed a lot. The cotton quilting fabric manufactured and specially designed for quilters is normally 44″ wide. There are a lot of different kinds of cotton available, but the fabric that works the best is quilter's cotton.

LINEN

Linen is a natural fabric that is woven like quilter's cotton but often has a looser weave. It has a great texture and it makes colors look rich, but it can be a little wiggly to work with. We used linen for the Cut-Away Rug (page 94).

FLANNEL

Flannel fabric has a brushed surface that feels warm and fuzzy. The type of flannel used for quilting is usually made of cotton. The texture of flannel makes it great for baby quilts or extra snuggly quilts. We used bright and cheery flannels in the Rag Quilt (page 78).

CUDDLE

Cuddle is a synthetic plush fabric that is super soft and, as its name says, cuddly. This fabric is best for quilts with larger pieces, since it is stretchy and a little harder to work with than cotton. It is also wider than cotton fabrics, usually 60″ wide. You can see the Cuddle fabric we used in the Cuddle Quilt (page 120).

After you decide on the type of fabric, you are ready for the funnest part: picking out the colors and prints.

PRECUT FABRICS

Precuts are bundles of cut fabric sold as a package. They are usually cotton. They make quilting fun and easy since the cutting is already done. Precuts come in various sizes. The selection of coordinated fabrics is often straight from the fabric manufacturer, or created by the seller. You can find precuts in different sizes of squares, strips, or even triangles. We used charm packs for the Charmed Quilt (page 72).

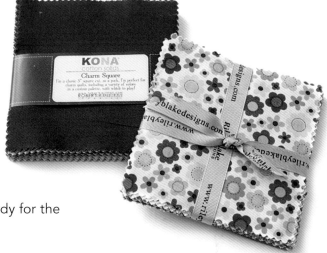

" My mom let me pick out almost all the fabrics for the projects in this book. She told me to pick what I liked since I would be the one keeping the quilts. You should do the same. Pick fabrics you like, and don't worry if they go together or not. This is your quilt! "

Cloe

Photo by Briana Gray

BATTING

Although it sounds like it has to do with baseball, *batting* is actually the soft layer in the middle of quilts that makes them warm and comfy. Batting is what makes it a quilt instead of just a blanket. You can buy batting by the yard or already packaged in different sizes.

Just as with fabric, there are many different kinds of batting. They range from thin to thick and can be made of different materials. Battings made from polyester or cotton are the most common types used.

For two of the projects in this book, we used a special insulated batting to keep heat or cold in or out of the finished item (Insul-Fleece, available from C&T Publishing).

Here are a few terms to help you understand more about batting:

LOFT

Loft is the puffiness or thickness of the batting. Batting labeled *low loft* is thinner and easier to manage; *high loft* is thicker and best for quilts that won't have a lot of quilting stitches sewn through all the thick layers.

DRAPE

Drape refers to how the batting hangs, whether it's stiff or more fluid. For a cuddly throw or quilt, you may want batting with a drape, but for a school supply roll, you'd want a stiffer batting.

WHAT KIND OF BATTING TO USE

Just as with fabric, it depends on what you like. Try out different kinds and see what you like best or what works for your project. For example, polyester batting has good drape but can vary by brand and style. I like to use a thin polyester batting. It's easy to work with and I love how it feels.

are you ready?

Now that you know what supplies you need, it's time to get started. In the next section, we'll walk you through the process from start to finish, including cutting the fabric, sewing, and using different quilting techniques.

making a quilt

In this section, Cloe and I will walk you through the steps of making a quilt, from start to finish. If you're a new quilter, it's a good idea to take the time to read through this section before you get started. While working on the projects in this book, you can use this section as a reference if you have any questions.

the projects

Each project shows what the quilt or quilted object will look like when it's finished. It also lists the supplies needed and gives you step-by-step instructions to make it.

Read the directions all the way through before you start. It will help you make sure you understand the whole process and know what you will need along the way.

the supplies

The project instructions will tell you what supplies you will need to make the project. Most quilting supplies can be found at local quilt shops, at craft stores, or online. Don't be afraid to ask for help finding the right products. Make sure you have all the supplies you need before you start working on the project.

appliqué

The word may sound fancy, but *appliqué* is simply attaching a smaller piece of fabric on top of a larger one. There are many different ways to do appliqué, but for the projects in this book we use a simple technique called *raw-edge appliqué*.

Raw-Edge Appliqué

For this method, all you do is place the appliqué piece on top of the background fabric and sew around it, close to the edges. "Raw" means the cut edges of the appliqué are exposed and will fray slightly, which adds texture.

We will also use raw-edge *fusible* appliqué, another simple method in which you use a special adhesive and your iron to attach the appliqué to the background fabric.

cutting

Now it's time to cut up the beautiful fabric you picked out. This is where your rotary cutter, ruler, and cutting mat (see Rotary Cutter, Ruler, and Cutting Mat, page 10) come in handy! Let's discuss how to use them before you cut the fabric.

Tips for Using a Rotary Cutter

Rotary cutting takes practice, and you should be very careful; ask an adult for help.

- You will use the measurement lines on the ruler to help you cut the fabric pieces exactly the size you need. For instance, if you need to cut a 2″ strip, line up the 2″ mark on the ruler with the straightened, cut edge of the fabric.

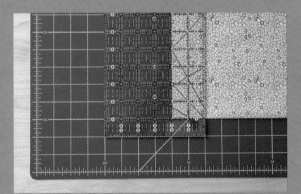

Line up ruler

- With your left hand, hold down the ruler firmly so it won't shift during cutting. This is also the hand that you need to put the safety glove on (see the safety glove photos, pages 10 and 11).

> *"I am left-handed, so I hold the rotary cutter in my left hand and hold the ruler with my right."*
>
> *Cloe*

- Open the rotary cutter, and slowly and firmly roll the rotary cutter forward, away from you and right alongside the edge of the ruler.

Rotary cutting (right-handed)

- Do not move the rotary cutter back and forth while cutting. You will get a better cut if you only roll it forward.

- Lock or slide the blade closed on the rotary cutter. Get into the habit of covering the blade so you do it automatically after each use, even if for a short time. The cutting gloves help protect your hand while you're cutting, but the rotary cutter's blade is very sharp, so don't leave it lying around exposed when not in use.

Squaring Up the Edges of the Fabric

Let's cut some fabric!

Most cotton fabrics are 44″ from selvage to selvage. The selvages are the finished edges of the fabric.

1. Lay the fabric on your cutting mat. Fold it so the selvages are lined up on top of each other, creating 2 layers of fabric. The cut edge may not line up at this point, but adjust the fabric until it lies flat.

2. Adjust the fabric on the cutting mat so the selvages are lined up with a grid line on the cutting mat, making it nice and straight. The selvages should be the top edges of the fabric, and the fold should be on the bottom.

3. Once the selvage edges are straight, you will need to trim one of the side edges straight, so your pieces can start out nice and straight.

If you are right-handed, you will trim the right edge. If you are left-handed, you will trim the left edge.

4. Align the ruler as shown and trim one side edge even. This is called *squaring up* the fabric. Once the fabric is squared up, you're ready to proceed to the cutting directions for the project.

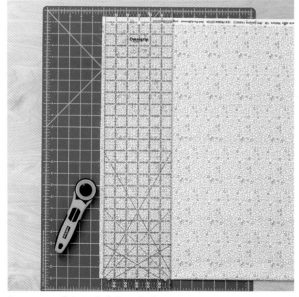

Square up fabric (left-handed).

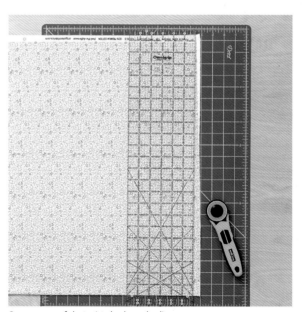

Square up fabric (right-handed).

Cutting Strips, Squares, and Rectangles

CUTTING STRIPS

The instructions for each project (in Hands-On Practice, page 46, and Projects, page 64) will tell you what you need to cut. Let's look at the Rag Quilt (page 78) for an example. The cutting directions say this:

> Cut 21 strips 5″ × width of fabric.

Line up the squared-up edge of the fabric (see Squaring Up the Edges of the Fabric, page 19) with the 5″ mark on your ruler and cut the fabric with the rotary cutter, from the bottom (fold) toward the top (selvages). You will have a 5″-wide strip from selvage to selvage (the width of the fabric).

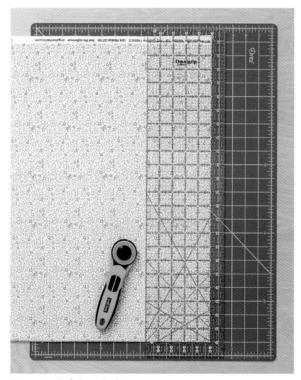

Cut strip (left-handed).

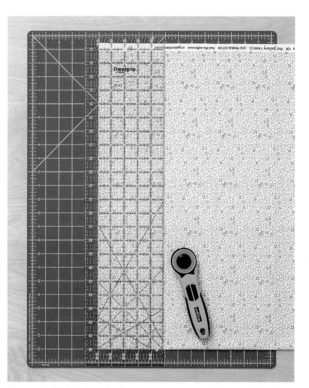

Cut strip (right-handed).

TIP: Don't unfold the strips quite yet. Leaving them folded will make the next step easier.

CUTTING SQUARES

The second part of the cutting instructions in our example says this:

> Subcut into 168 squares 5″ × 5″.

note ──────────────────────────────────

Subcut means that you are cutting the strips again, into smaller pieces.

1. Carefully pick up the folded strip and turn it so it sits horizontally on the cutting mat, so the selvages are on the side (on the right side if cutting right-handed; on the left side if cutting left-handed). Line up the strip with the lines on the mat.

2. Place the ruler about ½″ from the edge with the selvages and trim off the selvages.

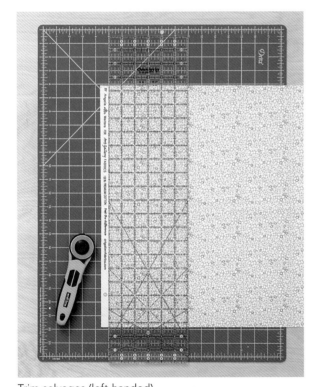

Trim selvages (left-handed).

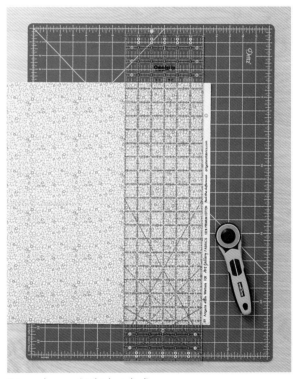

Trim selvages (right-handed).

note ──────────────────────────────────

The selvages are handy for making sure the fabric is folded straight, but you don't want to use them in the project. They are woven differently and will not look or act the same as the rest of the fabric in your project. Cutting off the selvages now will keep them out of your project.

3. Turn the fabric around so the cut edge is on the left for right-handers (right for left-handers). Line up the ruler's 5″ line with the cut edge of the fabric and cut through both layers. You will have 2 squares that are 5″ × 5″.

Continue cutting strips and squares like this, until you have as many squares as the project instructions say you need.

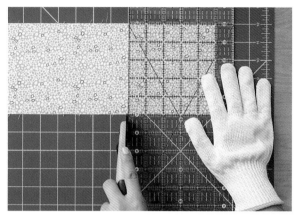
Cut squares (left-handed).

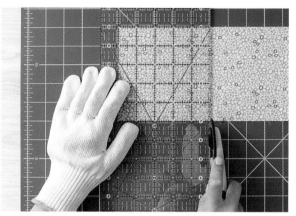
Cut squares (right-handed).

CUTTING RECTANGLES

Sometimes the project instructions may say something like:

Cut 2 rectangles 5″ × 12½″.

You will cut these almost the same way as you cut strips and squares.

Start by cutting a strip the width of the smaller measurement, in this case 5″ (see Cutting Strips, page 20). (Remember to trim off the selvages.) Line up the ruler's 12½″ line with the edge of the fabric and cut through both layers. You will have 2 rectangles that are 5″ × 12½″.

note —————

If you only need one rectangle, open the strip and cut through only a single layer of fabric.

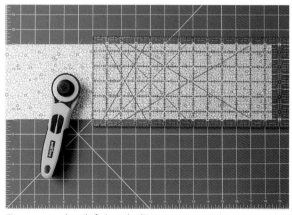
Cut rectangles (left-handed).

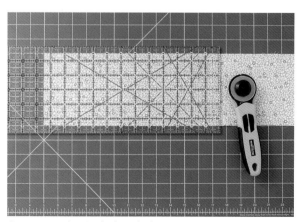
Cut rectangles (right-handed).

Make sure you follow all the cutting instructions, so that the pieces needed for the project will fit together when it's time to sew.

Cutting Wide Strips, Squares, and Rectangles

If the strip, square, or rectangle is wider than your ruler, tape two rulers together with masking tape or painter's tape, and use them as a single ruler.

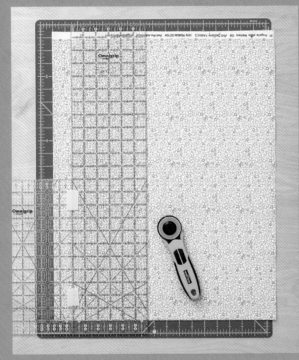

Cut a wide strip.

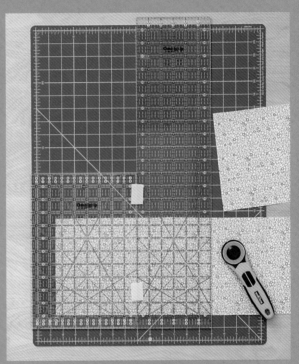

Cut a wide rectangle.

TIP: In some cases, when you need to cut a large measurement, you can simply fold the fabric to get twice the measurement. For example, to cut a 15″-wide strip, fold the fabric and use the 7½″ mark. But if you want to cut without folding the fabric, taping the ruler is accurate.

pressing

It is very important to press properly with an iron when the instructions tell you to press. It helps the patchwork fit together more accurately.

After you have sewn two pieces together, open the pieces with the right side up and press with the iron, pressing the seam allowances toward the darker fabric. (If there is no darker fabric, the project instructions in this book will tell you what direction to press the seams.)

note

Please be very careful when using an iron. If you haven't used an iron before, ask for an adult's help. Always unplug it when you're finished.

TIP: Be sure to press the pieces open so there are no tucks or pleats near the seam allowance. You want the pieces to be opened all the way.

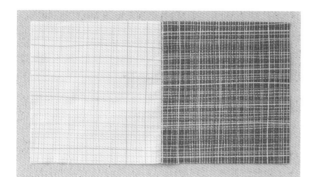

Right side

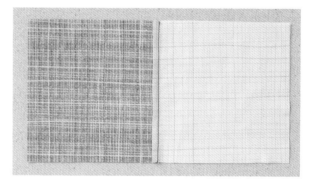

Wrong side

sewing

Now that you have cut your fabrics into a lot of little pieces, it's time to sew them all together. The projects have step-by-step instructions telling you what pieces to sew together.

Sewing a ¼˝ Seam Allowance

Most quilts use a seam allowance of ¼˝. A *seam allowance* is the distance between the stitching line and the edge of the fabric.

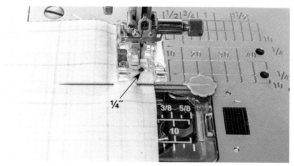

The seam allowance is the distance between the needle and the fabric edge.

Most sewing machines have a ¼″ presser foot, sometimes called a *patchwork foot*, that will help you get the correct seam allowance. Just line up the edge of the fabric with the edge of the ¼″ presser foot.

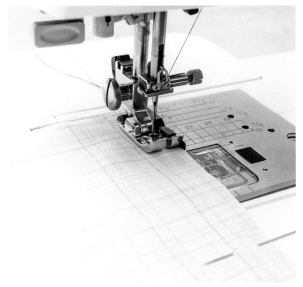

Sewing with ¼″ presser foot

note _____

If you don't have a ¼″ presser foot for your sewing machine, place several layers of masking tape or painter's tape together to make a thick stack. Then tape it exactly ¼″ from the needle. Align the edge of your fabric with this line when you sew your pieces together. Be sure to use painter's tape or a masking tape that will come off cleanly.

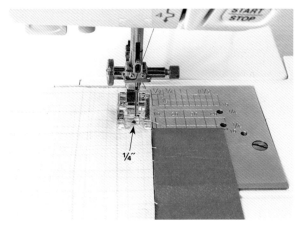

¼″

Using masking tape to mark ¼″ seam

Sewing Pieces of Fabric Together ------------------------------

1. Place 2 pieces of fabric with the front sides (right sides) together, so all you see is the back of the fabric (wrong side). The raw edges of the fabric should match up.

2. Using straight pins, pin the pieces along the side you want to sew together. This holds the fabric and keeps the pieces from shifting as you are sewing.

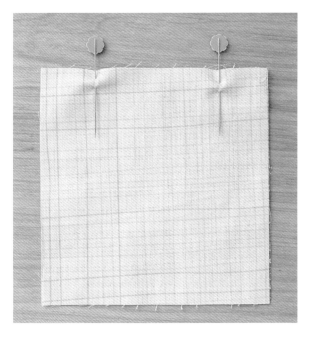

3. Lift the presser foot, place the pinned pieces under the foot of the sewing machine, lower the presser foot, and carefully sew them together. Make sure to remove the pins—do not sew over them!

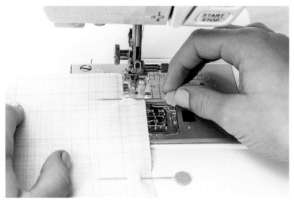

Remove pins as you sew.

note _____

If you're left-handed, you might find it more natural to have the pins face the other way.

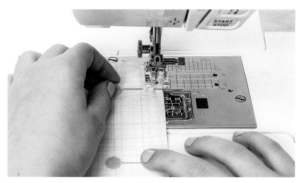

Remove pins as you sew (left-handed).

4. Carefully press the block open (see Pressing, page 24). Using a hot iron, carefully press the seam to one side. Pressing will make it easier to join these pieces to other pieces later.

Making the Quilt Top

The next part of the project instructions will tell you how to assemble the quilt top (the top layer of the quilt). There will often be an assembly diagram showing how pieces fit together. Many of the quilts in this book are pieced in rows, and the rows are made up of blocks.

Here is how Cloe sews together the pieces of her quilt tops.

1. Lay out the blocks in rows. Check that they are in the order you want them.

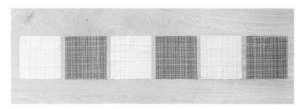

Lay out blocks in order.

2. Sew the blocks in 1 row together in pairs. Press the seams toward the darker fabric. If there isn't a darker fabric, the instructions in this book will tell you which way to press (see Pressing, page 24).

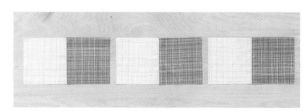

Sew blocks in pairs.

" *Sewing the blocks together in groups of two makes it easier to keep track of them.* "

Cloe

3. Sew the units together until all the blocks in the row are sewn together. Press the seams toward the darker fabric.

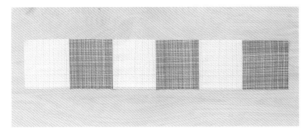

Sew pairs into row.

4. Repeat Steps 2 and 3 for each row.

5. After the rows are pieced (sewn together), sew the rows together. Place 2 rows together, with the right sides facing each other, and pin, matching seamlines.

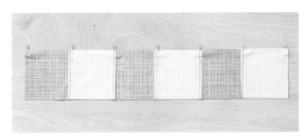

Pin rows together.

This will give you nicely matched intersections where the seams come together.

Pin near intersection.

note _____

Since you pressed the seams toward the dark side, the seams position themselves in opposite directions where they come together. This is called *nesting* the seams, and the result is better-looking intersections.

6. Sew the 2 rows together. Press the row seam in one direction.

7. Sew the rows together in pairs, and then sew the pairs together. For this sample quilt, we pressed blocks toward the dark fabric; but in general, press the row seams all in the same direction.

8. Keep joining the rows until the quilt top is put together.

quilting and finishing

Yay! The quilt top is pieced and now it's time for another fun part … the quilting! There are several different ways to quilt a quilt top. In this section, you will learn how to prepare the layers of a quilt and how to use different quilting techniques.

piecing the backing

Before you can make your *quilt sandwich* (a quilt top and a quilt back with batting in between), you need to get the fabric for the back ready. The quilt backing should be larger than the quilt top. This will make it easier to hold the quilt when you start quilting. Cloe and I like to have about 2″–3″ extra on all sides, or less for small projects.

Most projects in this book are small enough for you to use just one piece of fabric for the backing. But for larger projects, such as the

Charmed Quilt (page 72), you can sew two pieces together to make the backing big enough.

To piece the backing, cut the fabric in half and sew the long sides using a ½″ seam. (Figure A)

Figure A

If you don't like the look of the seam going across the middle, use three sections. The fabric requirements given in the projects allow for either piecing method. (Figure B)

There is another option. Modern quilts often use irregular placement of blocks, and you can use this method in the backing. For example, you could sew leftover blocks and strips to create an interesting backing. (Figure C)

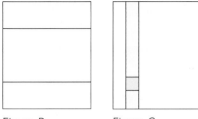

Figure B   Figure C

layering the quilt sandwich and basting the quilt

Before you can get to the quilting, you have to make a sandwich. Not the kind you eat—you are going to make a quilt sandwich. As we mentioned, a *quilt sandwich* is made using the three layers of the quilt: the top, the batting, and the backing. This step is important because you don't want the layers to shift as you are quilting.

Fusible batting is like regular batting except it has a glue-like substance on it to hold the layers of your quilt sandwich together while you are quilting. Make sure to read the instructions on the fusible batting package before you start.

1. On a large, flat surface, such as the floor, lay out the quilt backing, right side down. Make sure it's smooth and flat.

" *There are different ways to baste the layers together, but we are going to show you my favorite way, using fusible batting.* "

Cloe

note _____

To make the basting process easier, the backing and batting should be larger than the quilt top. For smaller projects, it's okay to have a small extra amount, like 1″, because you can easily see and handle the entire quilt sandwich. For larger projects, it's safer to have 2″ or 3″ extra on all sides.

2. Place the fusible batting on top of the backing. It's a little sticky, but that just helps it stay in place.

3. Lay the quilt top on top of the batting so that the right side is facing up. Smooth it out and make sure all the layers are wrinkle-free and flat.

4. To "glue" the layers together, use an iron to press the quilt top. Follow the instructions on the fusible interfacing, and use the recommended heat and steam settings, and amount of pressing time. Turn the sandwich over and press the back side. As the iron moves over the quilt sandwich, the heat melts the glue on the batting and fuses the layers together.

If you don't like using fusible batting, or if you don't have any, here are 2 more options:

- You can baste the quilt sandwich together using safety pins spaced about 6˝ apart across the entire surface.

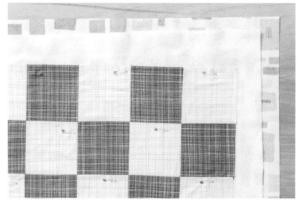

- You can use basting spray. Be sure to follow the instructions on the can.

quilting

It's not a quilt until it's quilted! *Quilting*, as a noun, refers to the stitches holding the layers of a quilt together. It is functional because it's needed to hold the quilt together, but the quilting method and design you choose is where you can express your creativity!

note

Even though each project in this book has a suggested quilting technique, you might want to use a different technique. Think about how the object will be used, what tools are available, and do what feels right for your project.

The projects in this book use three different quilting techniques: hand quilting, tie quilting, and machine quilting. Cloe and I will show you how to do all of them!

Tie quilting

Hand quilting

Machine quilting

Hand Quilting

Hand quilting

For hand quilting, you use a needle and thread to hand sew stitches through all three basted layers. It takes longer than the other quilting techniques, but the result could be exactly the look and texture you want!

note

The Appliqué Letter Pillow (page 84) was hand quilted.

HAND QUILTING SUPPLIES

THREAD

There are different kinds of thread you can use for hand quilting.

Hand-quilting thread is made especially for hand quilting—the spool will be labeled. It's thicker than regular sewing thread. Of the three thread choices we'll talk about, this thread allows the hand quilting to blend in more with the quilt, especially if you match the color to your project.

Embroidery thread is normally used for embroidery projects, but it can be used for hand quilting, too. This is the kind of thread we used on the Appliqué Letter Pillow (page 84).

Perle cotton thread is a heavy, soft thread that resembles yarn when you see it up close but is not as thick or fuzzy—in  fact, it is smooth and silky. Using this thread will make your quilting really show up!

NEEDLES

The needle you use for hand quilting depends on the type of thread you decide to use. If you are using hand-quilting thread, you can use any regular sewing needle. Needles are often labeled as embroidery needles or darning needles. For best results, though, quilters use a *between* needle, size 10. But if that looks too small to handle, you could start with a size 6 or 7 between quilting needle.

For embroidery thread or perle cotton, you will need a needle with a large enough eye for the thicker thread or for multiple strands. Embroidery needles, also called *sharps*, have a longer eye to make threading easier. The needle size depends on the thread. For example, a size 5 embroidery needle worked well with the perle cotton used in the Appliqué Letter Pillow (page 84). It could also be used with the six-strand embroidery floss Cloe used to tie the Charmed Quilt (page 72).

QUILTING HOOP

A quilting hoop holds the layers in place and can make it a little easier to hand quilt. If you don't have one, don't worry! They aren't really necessary for smaller projects.

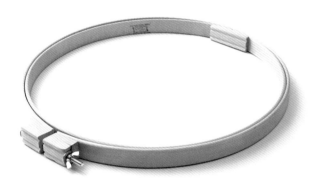

THIMBLE

This tool fits on your finger and will help you push the needle through the quilt layers. Wearing a thimble feels strange at first, but if you decide you like hand quilting, it's worth getting used to the feeling.

HOW TO HAND QUILT

1. Cut a piece of thread about 18″ long. Thread one end through the eye of the needle. Tie a knot at the other end, also called the *thread tail*.

2. From the top side of the quilt sandwich, insert the needle about ½″ away from where you want to start quilting. Pull the threaded needle through the batting, but not the back of the quilt, and come out the top where you want to start the quilting. Give the thread a little tug to pull the knot through the quilt top. This will hide the knot in the batting; this is called *burying the knot*.

> **TIP:** For hand quilting with perle cotton or multiple strands of embroidery thread, don't make the start knot huge because it would be hard to tug it through. A single knot will work fine.

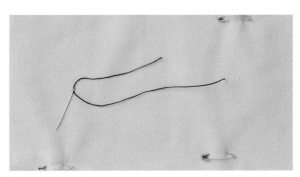
Bury the start knot.

3. To start making quilting stitches, push the needle down through the quilt sandwich a short distance from where it came through the quilt top.

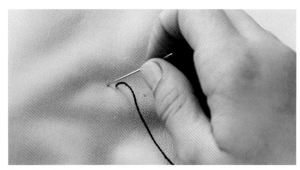
Needle down

4. As soon as the tip of the needle starts to come out the bottom side, angle the needle back up toward the top. Pull the needle through the top to complete 1 stitch.

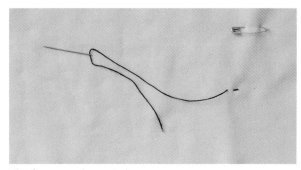
The first complete stitch

note

This pattern of evenly spaced stitches is called a *running stitch*. As you get more comfortable hand quilting, you can place a few stitches on the needle before you pull the needle through.

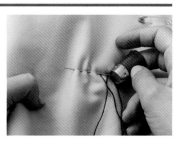

5. Keep making running stitches, working your way across the quilt using the same needle and thread.

6. When you've used up almost all your thread, make a small knot about ¼″ from the top of the quilt.

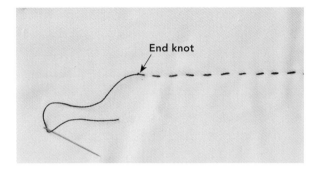

7. Pull the knot through the top layer and batting only, and snip off the extra thread, leaving the end knot buried in the batting.

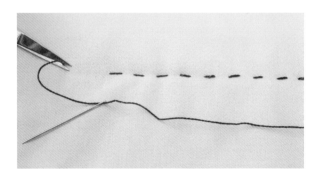

8. Repeat with new lengths of thread until you are finished with the quilting.

note _____

You can try to keep the stitches all the same size, but don't worry too much about it. It doesn't have to be perfect!

WHAT DESIGNS SHOULD I HAND QUILT?

The great thing about quilting is that you can use it to create designs on the quilt. Two different design ideas are straight-line quilting and echo quilting.

STRAIGHT-LINE QUILTING

In the Appliqué Letter Pillow (page 84) we quilted straight lines about ¼″ away from the seams. This is an easy and classic design for hand quilting.

Straight-line hand quilting

ECHO QUILTING

Try quilting lines that echo a shape on the quilt. On the flower pillow in Change It Up! (page 89) we echoed the shape of the flower with the quilting. Such a fun look!

Echo quilting

Tie Quilting

Tie quilting

Tie quilting is a quick way to finish the quilt and the easiest of the quilting options.

note

This is the quilting technique we used for the Charmed Quilt (page 72).

TIE QUILTING SUPPLIES

THREAD

There are different kinds of thread you can use for tie quilting.

We talked about using embroidery thread for hand quilting (Hand Quilting Supplies, page 32), but it is strong enough for tie quilting, too. We used all six strands of embroidery thread in the Charmed Quilt (page 72).

Perle cotton thread is a soft, thicker thread with a sheen that will make your tie quilting shine! You would use a single strand of perle cotton for tying.

NEEDLES

A good needle for tying your quilt could be the same as what we discussed for hand quilting (see Needles, (page 33). If you think a thicker needle will be easier, try a crewel needle, size 10 or 12. It's bigger but not so big that it will leave holes in your work.

HOW TO TIE A QUILT

1. Thread a needle, but don't make a knot at the end. Push the needle from the top of the quilt to the back of the quilt, through all 3 layers.

2. Insert the needle about ¼˝ away from where the thread came through the back of the quilt, and push it through to the top of the quilt.

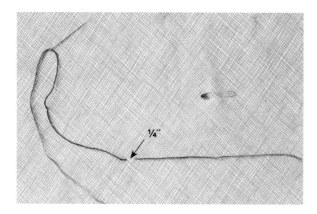

3. Pull the thread through until the tail end of the thread is a couple of inches from the quilt top.

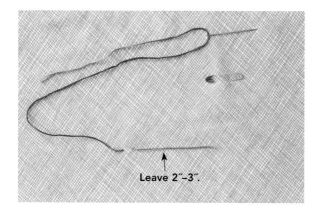

4. Make another stitch directly on top of the first stitch by going in the first hole and out the second.

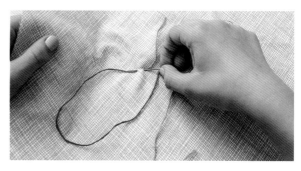

5. Pull the needle through and cut the thread a couple of inches from the quilt top.

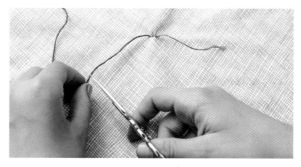

6. Tie the ends together in a double knot. Trim the ends ½˝ from the quilt top.

7. Work your way around the quilt tying knots.

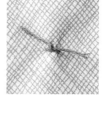

You can put as many knots as you would like, wherever you like. On the Charmed Quilt (page 72) we put a knot in the center of each square. You could also put knots in the corners or rows. It's up to you! Just be sure you have enough to keep the layers secure through using, washing, and drying. Your batting package should tell you the maximum spacing you can have. You can always add more ties.

Machine Quilting

You can also use your sewing machine to quilt the layers together. This is called *machine quilting* and is usually the fastest quilting method. We will talk about two different ways to machine quilt: straight-line quilting and free-motion quilting.

Not only is machine quilting fast, but it usually creates more durable stitches that are smaller and closer together. So if you're deciding what quilting method to use to finish a project, think about how the quilted project will be used. For the Quilted Water Bottle Holder (page 58) we used machine quilting, which made a sturdier result.

HOW TO MACHINE QUILT

1. Put the quilt sandwich under the presser foot of your sewing machine. For bigger quilts, you may need to roll up the sides to get it to fit in.

> **TIP:** When machine quilting on a regular sewing machine, we like to start in the center and work our way out. This helps prevent tucks or puckers from forming.

2. Starting with the needle in the up position, lower and raise the needle to pull up the bobbin thread to the top.

3. Set the stitch length very small (about 0.5) and make a few stitches in the same place to hold the thread in place. Trim the loose ends of the thread. Be careful not to cut the quilt top!

" *Some quilters like to tie the ends of the thread and bury them in the quilt, but I find that this method works best for me!* "

Cloe

4. Begin quilting through the layers of the quilt, working your way around the quilt.

Machine Quilting Tips *from Cloe*

1. Start small. The first time you try machine quilting, start with a smaller project. This will let you get the hang of machine quilting without having to work with a large quilt.

2. Get a boost. My mom's sewing table is a little high for me, so I have to sit on a higher chair when machine quilting. That keeps my back from getting sore and also makes the quilting easier.

3. Relax. I used to get so frustrated when I first started machine quilting, but my mom kept telling me to relax and have fun. The quilting probably will not be perfect, but that is okay! The most important thing is getting it finished!

Photo by Briana Gray

Straight-Line Machine Quilting

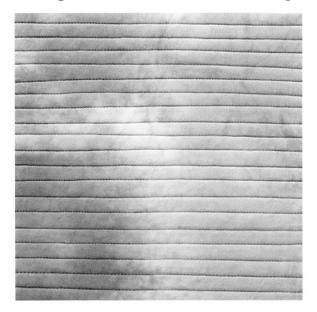

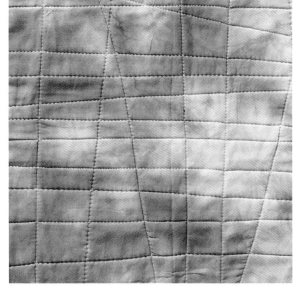

If you have a walking foot for your sewing machine, use it for straight-line machine quilting. A walking foot is great because it helps pull the quilt through the machine as you sew. This makes the quilting a little easier and helps prevent tucks and puckers in your quilt as you machine quilt.

A walking foot comes with some newer sewing machines, but it can also be bought separately. The feed dogs on your machine help guide the lower fabric; the walking foot acts like feed dogs for the top fabric.

You can only quilt straight lines and gentle curves with a walking foot.

If your machine has decorative stitches, they can be used for quilting straight lines and gentle curves.

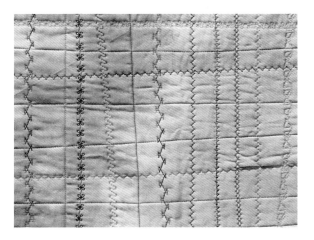

To get your feet wet with straight-line machine quilting, the Pot Holders (page 48) and Place Mats (page 52) are great projects to start with. They are both small enough so you can focus on the quilting. You can mark stitching lines if you want with a water-soluble fabric marker, or you can just quilt randomly.

Free-Motion Machine Quilting

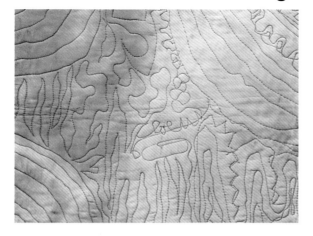

If you want to go beyond straight-line quilting and sew free-form shapes and curves with your sewing machine, you'll love free-motion quilting. It will open up a new world.

You need to make some adjustments on your sewing machine to prepare for free-motion quilting. You need to lower the *feed dogs*, the teeth that grip and move the fabric as you sew. With free-motion quilting, you control the fabric and your movements create the quilting design. It's like drawing, except that the paper moves and the pencil stays still—think of your fabric as paper and the needle and thread as your pencil.

> ----- **TIP:** Get to know your sewing machine! Read the manual to find out how to lower the feed dogs and change the presser foot.

For the presser foot, you'll need a free-motion quilting foot (or darning foot).

This foot glides across the fabric, giving you freedom to move the quilt around. This movement lets you quilt a lot of different designs, such as swirls and loops, that you couldn't do with the walking foot.

When you press the foot pedal, the needle goes up and down. It is up to you to move the quilt sandwich. Remember, the quilt fabric can move in any direction, but it takes practice to move the quilt around smoothly.

FREE-MOTION QUILTING SUPPLIES

Quilting gloves will help you grip the quilt sandwich, making it easier to move.

A Supreme Slider attaches to your sewing machine and has a slick surface that helps the quilt sandwich move more easily.

Most sewing machines have an optional extension table you can buy that makes the base of your sewing machine larger. It holds more of the quilt, making it easier to move around while you're machine quilting.

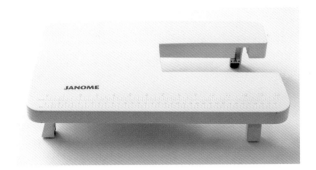

HOW TO DO FREE-MOTION QUILTING

Practice drawing a design on paper and then give it a try using your sewing machine. Why? Because drawing it on paper makes hand-brain connections that will give you a head start in machine quilting. Then once you're sitting at the sewing machine, you'll have better intuition for the drawing part.

Remember that the feed dogs are down, so you are in control of the stitch length. Sew slowly and steadily, and try not to jerk the quilt. If you forget to move, there will be lots of tiny stitches in one place. If you move too fast, the stitches will be large. But don't worry too much about how your first efforts look. You'll be amazed at how different your second or third try looks, compared with your first time.

If your machine has a needle-down feature, use it when you stop quilting so that your quilt sandwich stays in place. There is no need to pivot your work because you can move in any direction. Try to keep the top of your practice piece horizontal as you move around.

note

If your stitches don't look so great, you might be the only person to notice because you are holding it 2″ from your nose. Don't get trapped into thinking it must be perfect. It will still look fine in the project. Once you get the hang of it and you want to quilt everything in sight, just relax and remember to take your time!

TIP: Make small quilt sandwiches out of leftover scraps to practice on. Then move up to free-motion quilting on a smaller project such as a place mat to help you get the hang of it. Then you'll be ready to work on larger projects … like quilts!

 Here are some things I've learned about free-motion quilting.

- *Practice really helps, so if I don't like the quilting, I try it again.*
- *The setup takes time, but once you're set, it's really fun!*
- *If you can turn down the speed on the sewing machine, that may help.*

WHAT FREE-MOTION DESIGNS SHOULD I QUILT?

It helps to think of free-motion quilting as doodling with a pencil. The only difference is that you are using thread instead of a pencil. Some easy, beginner free-motion quilting designs include the meander and loopy meander.

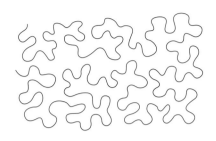 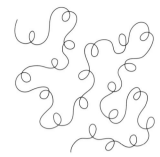

> *I am really lucky. My mom has a longarm quilting machine in her quilting studio. A longarm quilting machine is a really big machine that makes machine quilting easier.*
>
> *Every once in a while, she lets me quilt on it, too. I even quilted some of the projects in this book on it.*
>
> *Cloe*

Photos by Briana **Gray**

trimming and binding the quilt

Trimming

Once you finish the quilting, you need to trim the quilt. Trimming the quilt removes the extra batting and backing. This prepares the quilt for the binding. Using scissors or a rotary cutter, carefully cut next to the edge of the quilt top. Be careful not to cut the quilt top.

Binding

You are almost done! All that is left to do is the *binding*, or finishing the edges of the quilt so there are no raw edges.

There is more than one way to bind a quilt. We are going to show you our favorite way to make and put on the binding. It is called *continuous double-fold binding*.

MAKING THE BINDING

1. Cut the binding fabric into 2¼˝ strips. The project instructions will tell you how much fabric to cut.

2. Place the binding strips right sides together at a right angle.

3. Draw a diagonal line from corner to corner, as shown.

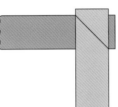

4. Sew on top of the line.

Sew on line.

5. Trim ¼˝ away from the seam, cutting off the corner.

Trim.

6. Open and press the seam to one side.

7. Repeat Steps 2–6 to sew all the strips together into 1 long strip.

8. Press the strip in half with the front (right) side showing.

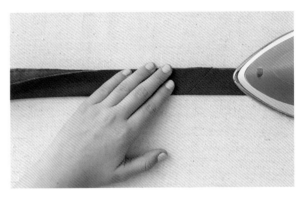

9. Work your way down the long strip until all the binding is pressed.

ATTACHING THE BINDING

1. Open the fold and cut one end of the binding diagonally.

2. Fold the raw edge under ¼″ and press.

3. Turn the quilt so the back of the quilt is facing up. Open the binding and line up the edge of the binding along the raw edge of the quilt. Start the binding in the middle of one side of the quilt, not at a corner.

4. Using a ¼″ seam allowance, sew 2″ from the beginning of the binding strip.

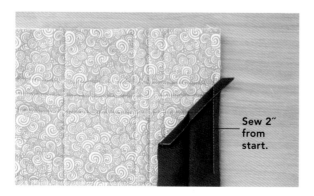

Sew 2″ from start.

5. Cut the thread. Fold the binding closed so the raw edges of the folded binding line up with the raw edge of the quilt.

6. Start sewing where you left off, through both layers of binding, and continue sewing a ¼″ seam. Stop sewing when you get ¼″ from the corner.

Leave open.

7. Cut the thread and rotate the quilt so that the next side is lined up with the presser foot.

8. Fold the binding straight up and away from the quilt.

9. Holding the binding underneath in place, fold it back down, so it is lined up with the edge of the quilt.

10. Start at the corner and sew along the next side of the quilt. Stop when you get ¼″ from the corner.

11. Repeat Steps 9 and 10, working your way around the quilt. Stop when you are about 3″ from where you started the binding.

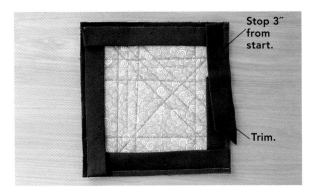

Stop 3″ from start.

Trim.

12. Trim the end of the binding so it overlaps the starting point by 1″.

13. Tuck the end of the binding into the opening at the starting point.

14. Sew the rest of the binding down.

15. Turn the quilt over so that the front faces up. Turn and fold the binding to the right side of the quilt. Pin. At the corners, fold one side down first and then fold the other side down.

16. Sew the binding down about ⅛″ from the folded edge.

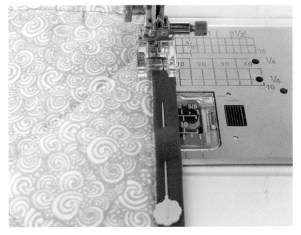

17. Work your way around the quilt, turning corners as in Step 15.

Hands-On Practice

This section includes three projects to help build up the skills needed for making quilts. Remember that you can go back to the previous chapters if you get stuck on any of the steps.

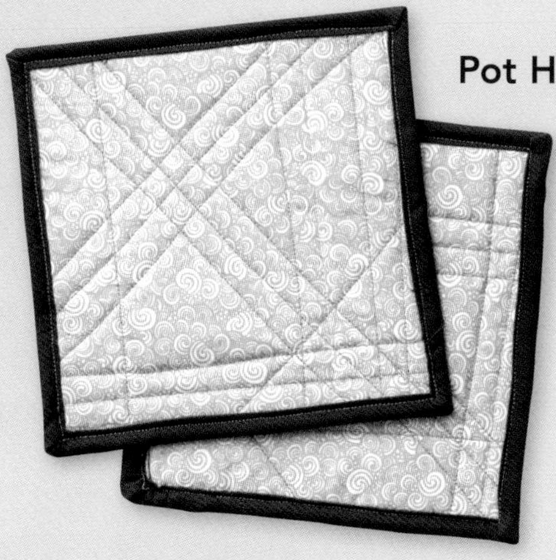

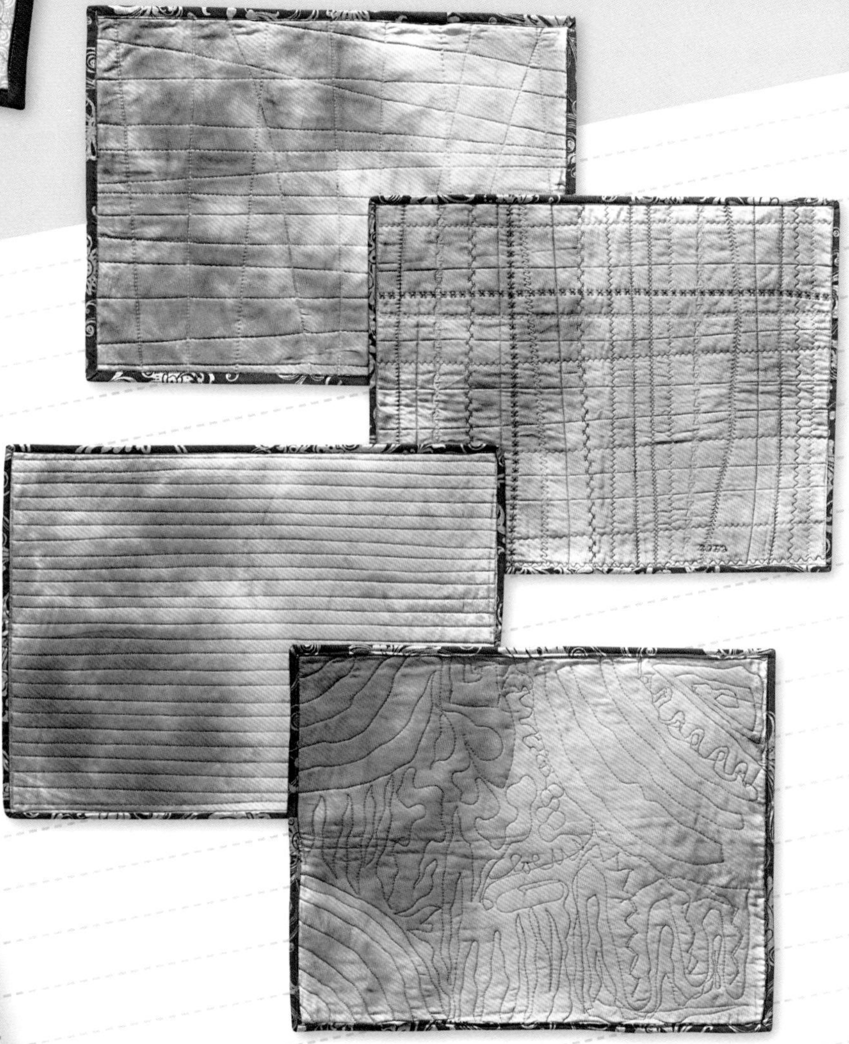

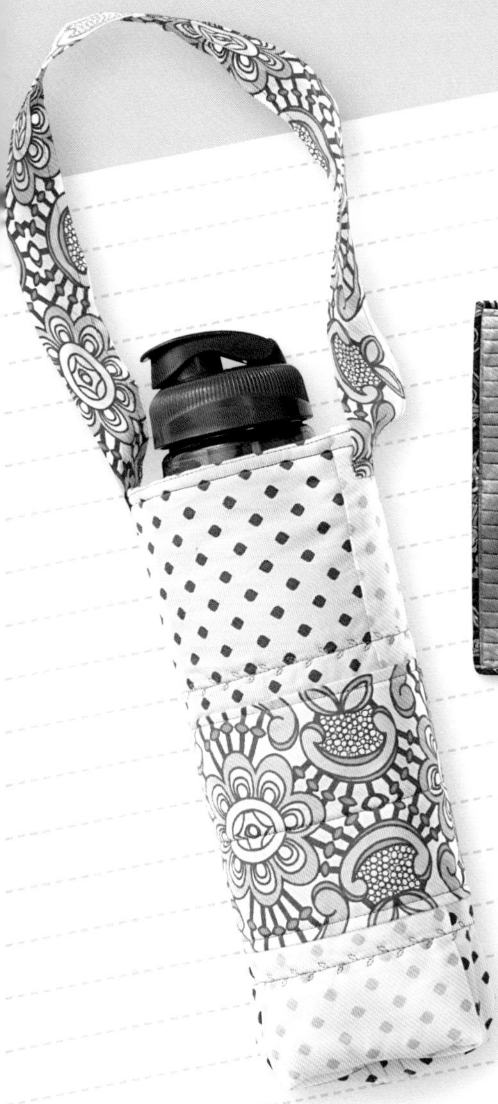

pot holders

Read Making a Quilt (page 16) before you start this project.

WHAT YOU'LL NEED

Makes 2 pot holders.

- **Fabric:** ⅓ yard (2 pot holders, front and back)

- **Binding:** ¼ yard

- **Insulated batting:** 2 pieces 8″ × 8″ (I used Insul-Fleece by C&T Publishing; if you don't have insulated batting, use cotton batting: 4 pieces 8″ × 8″.)

TECHNIQUES USED:

- Cutting (page 18)

- Layering the Quilt Sandwich and Basting the Quilt (page 29)

- Quilting (page 31)

- Trimming and Binding the Quilt (page 42)

In this project you will get to see the whole process of making quilts by making pot holders. Pot holders are really just small quilts! This is a fast and easy project, and it will help you get familiar with your sewing machine. You will practice basting, machine quilting, trimming, and binding a quilt.

cutting

Fabric:

Cut on the fold of the fabric to make 2 pieces approximately 12″ × 21″.

- From 1 piece, cut a strip 7″ × 21″; subcut into 2 squares 7″ × 7″ for the fronts of the pot holders.

- From the other piece, cut a strip 9″ × 21″; subcut into 2 squares 9″ × 9″* for the backs of the pot holders.

From binding fabric, cut 2 strips 2¼″ × width of fabric.

* Refer to Cutting Wide Strips, Squares, and Rectangles (page 23) for help.

making the pot holder

Use the Techniques Used list (page 48) to find more information if you need help.

1. Prepare the quilt sandwich by placing a 9″ × 9″ square of fabric face down (right side down) on a flat surface. Place one square of insulated batting or 2 squares of regular batting on top for the middle layer, and center the 7″ × 7″ square of fabric, right side facing up, on top of that.

2. Baste the layers together with 2 or 3 safety pins.

3. Machine quilt the layers together. Cloe quilted straight lines in random directions, but you could hand quilt or tie quilt instead.

4. Trim the batting and backing even with the 7″ × 7″ top piece of fabric.

5. Sew binding around the edges of the pot holder.

note _____

For a bigger quilt, we would plan the backing and batting to extend about 1″–2″ beyond the top on all sides, even more for longarm quilting. For the pot holders, we used ½″ extra at all sides, plenty for a mini-quilt!

My mom had me make pot holders when I was first learning how to quilt. She said it was just like a mini-quilt. The practice really helped me when it came time to make a larger quilt!

Cloe

place mats

Read Making a Quilt (page 16) before you start this project.

TECHNIQUES USED:

Cutting (page 18)

Pressing (page 24)

Layering the Quilt Sandwich and Basting the Quilt (page 29)

Quilting (page 31)

Trimming and Binding the Quilt (page 42)

This project is a great way to practice basting and machine quilting. Cloe and I will show you how to make a set of place mats and machine quilt them in many different ways. You can try each way or pick your favorite.

cutting

Cut 5 strips 2¼″ × 21″ for the binding strips.

note

This is the perfect project for trying out all different kinds and colors of threads. Using a bunch of wild, contrasting colors will help make your place mats unique!

FINISHED SIZE:
15½˝ × 20½˝

making the place mat

Use the Techniques Used list (page 52) to find more information if you need help.

Preparing the Layers

Layer and baste the quilt sandwich with backing, batting, and top fabric.

You are ready to start quilting!

Quilting the Place Mat

Try each machine quilting technique, or just choose your favorite!

TECHNIQUE #1: STRAIGHT-LINE QUILTING

Straight-line quilting is one of the easiest ways to practice machine quilting. The walking foot gives you more control of the fabric layers, and the small size of the place mat makes it easy to turn the project.

1. GET RANDOM

Instead of quilting straight, evenly spaced lines, you can give your quilts a crazier look by quilting lines in random directions. Try horizontal, vertical, and even diagonal!

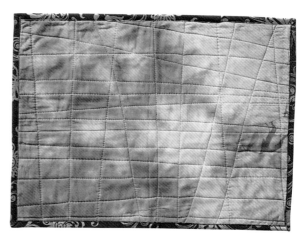

This is my favorite way to quilt straight lines. I don't have to worry about measuring or keeping them even!

Cloe

2. BE SQUARE

Who says straight lines have to be evenly spaced? Instead of random lines, try quilting a square that echoes around itself.

This is easy to do since the place mat is small enough to turn. To quilt an echoed square, start by quilting a small square toward the middle of the place mat. Then start echoing around and around the square. When you get to a corner, simply rotate the place mat and continue quilting.

Remember, you can add as many quilting lines as you want. The machine quilting adds firmness to the project because the stitches add body. So if your place mat seems too droopy, just add more machine quilting.

> **TIP:** To turn the corner, leave the needle down in the quilt sandwich. Lift the presser foot and carefully rotate the place mat. Lower the presser foot and continue quilting.

TECHNIQUE #2: DECORATIVE STITCHES

Of course, there is no reason to stick with straight stitches. Many sewing machines come with decorative stitches, which allow you to create an interesting quilting design. Some may require a change of presser foot, but many will still use the regular presser foot that's used for straight or zigzag stitching. Get to know your machine and use the place mat to try as many, or as few, of the decorative stitches as you would like.

> **TIP:** Refer to the owner's manual of your machine for instructions on how to change the presser foot and select decorative stitches.

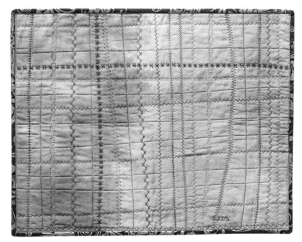

Decorative stitches can be a lot of fun to use on your place mat.

" *I absolutely loved picking out different stitches. I used almost all of them on my place mats!* "

TECHNIQUE #3
FREE-MOTION QUILTING

Why should your walking foot have all the fun? Trade it for your free-motion quilting foot and try quilting your place mats with some fun free-motion quilting designs.

> ----- **TIP:** Not sure what we are talking about? Refer to Free-Motion Machine Quilting (page 40).

Smaller projects, such as these place mats, are great for practicing free-motion quilting. Start with an easy, basic design and quilt it on your place mat. If you aren't sure what to quilt or you just want to practice first, try doodling on a piece of paper. Practicing on paper will help you develop the skills you'll need when you quilt on fabric!

If you can't pick just one design, try a bunch of your favorite designs. The most important thing is to just have fun with it!

Doodling is a great way to practice new free-motion quilting designs.

Finishing

Once you are finished with your place mat masterpieces, trim and bind them.

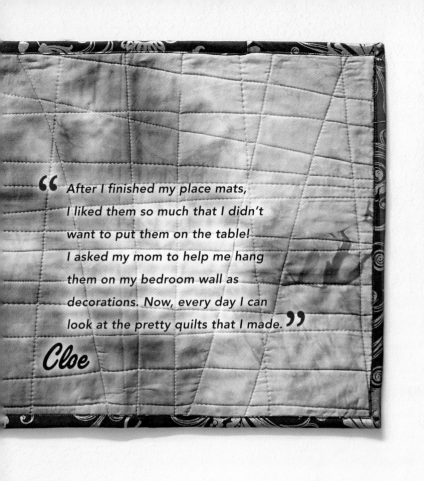

" After I finished my place mats,
I liked them so much that I didn't
want to put them on the table!
I asked my mom to help me hang
them on my bedroom wall as
decorations. Now, every day I can
look at the pretty quilts that I made. "

Cloe

quilted water bottle holder

Read Making a Quilt (page 16) before you start this project.

WHAT YOU'LL NEED

Medium blue dot: 1 fat quarter

Light blue dot: 1 fat quarter

Blue floral: 1 fat quarter

Backing: 1 fat quarter

Batting: Insul-Fleece 14″ × 14″ square

TECHNIQUES USED:

Cutting (page 18)

Pressing (page 24)

Sewing (page 24)

Layering the Quilt Sandwich and Basting the Quilt (page 29)

Quilting (page 31)

Trimming and Binding the Quilt (page 42)

notes

- A fat quarter is approximately 18″ × 21″.

- Insulated batting will help keep your drink cooler for longer. If you don't have any, you can use regular batting.

cutting

Medium and light blue dot:
Cut 3 squares 4½″ × 4½″ from each fabric.

Blue floral:
Cut 1 rectangle 4½″ × 12½″.

Cut 1 strip 4″ × 20″.

Backing:
Cut 1 square 14″ × 14″.*

* Refer to Cutting Wide Strips, Squares, and Rectangles (page 23) for help.

making the water bottle holder

Use the Techniques Used list (page 58) to find more information if you need help.

Sewing the Outer Layer

1. Sew a light blue square to opposite sides of a medium blue block. Press seams toward the darker square.

2. Sew a medium blue square to opposite sides of a light blue block. Press seams toward the darker square.

3. Sew a row to the top and bottom of the blue floral rectangle. Press seams toward the center.

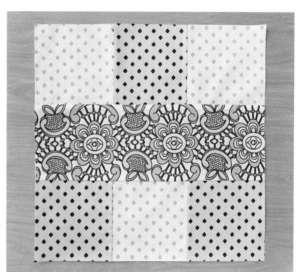

Layering, Basting, and Quilting

1. Using the backing and batting, prepare a quilt sandwich.

2. Quilt using your favorite quilting method.

 note

We chose to machine quilt ours. We used the walking foot to help keep the layers in place, and quilted straight lines.

3. Carefully trim away the extra batting and backing.

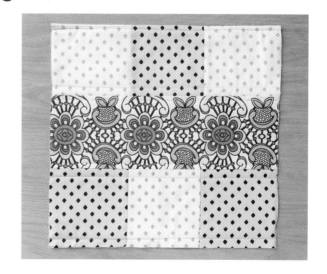

Finishing

1. Fold the top edge of the quilt toward the back and sew a line ¼˝ from the top. This makes the top edge look a little more finished.

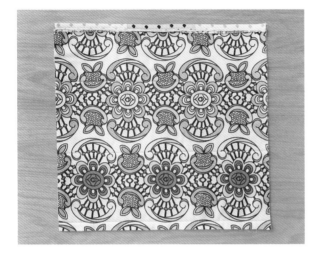

2. Fold the sandwich in half right sides together, and sew along the bottom and the side.

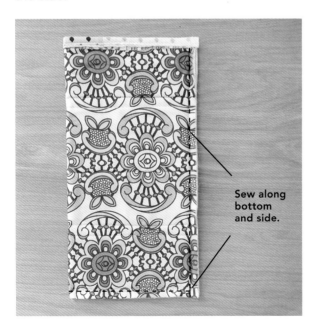

Sew along bottom and side.

3. From the bottom corner, cut out a 1½˝ × 1½˝ square. To do that, measure up and to the left 1½˝ from the bottom corner.

4. Repeat Step 3 for the other bottom corner.

5. Pinch each side of the cut-out square until a straight line forms. (For the corner with the side seam, you can match the seams.)

Pinch sides to create a straight seam.

note

For your water bottle holder to stand up, it needs a base. The sewing is a little tricky because of the thicknesses and small seams, but it is worth it to have a 3D object!

6. Pin together and sew ¼″ away from the raw edge.

7. Repeat Steps 5 and 6 to "box" the other corner.

8. Turn the water bottle holder right side out and set it aside. It's time to make the strap.

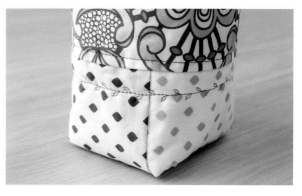

Making the Strap

1. Using the 4″ × 20″ strip of blue fabric, press under ½″ on both long sides.

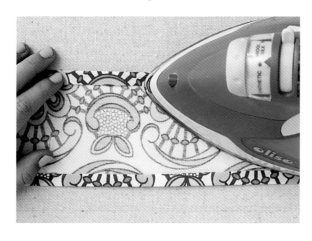

2. Fold the strap in half and match long edges. Press and pin.

3. Sew ¼″ away from the folded edges to finish the strap.

Attaching the Strap to the Holder

1. Place one end of the strap on the side of the water bottle holder, 1″ from the top edge. The strap should face down (you'll flip it in the next step). Pin. Sew the strap to the bottle holder.

2. Fold the strap up so the edge is tucked under. Pin. Sew ¼″ away to enclose the strap end.

3. Repeat Steps 1 and 2 to attach the other side of the strap to the other side of the bottle holder. Make sure the strap isn't twisted.

4. Grab your favorite bottled beverage and enjoy!

wanna customize it?

For a fun variation of the water bottle holder, try customizing it by writing your name on it with puffy paint before you start quilting. Make sure to let the paint dry before you start quilting.

Projects

Heart Ticker Tape Quilt   66

Charmed Quilt   72

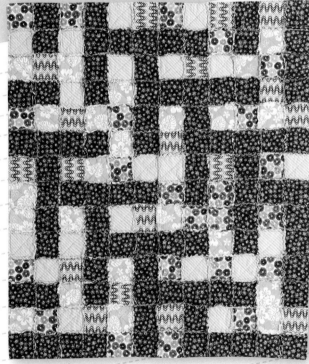

Rag Quilt   78

Appliqué Letter Pillow   84

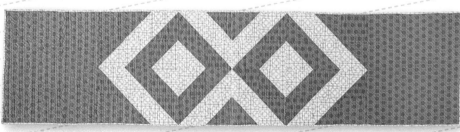

Bed Runner   90

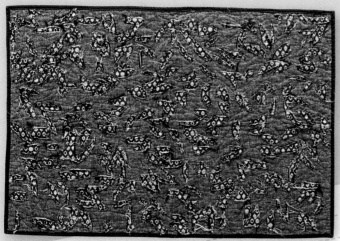

Cut-Away Rug 94

Signature Quilt 98

Ticker Tape Quilt 104

T-Shirt Quilt 114

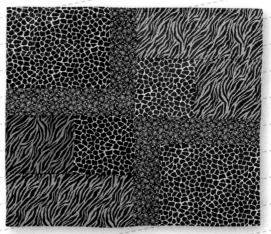

Cuddle Quilt 120

heart ticker tape quilt

Read Making a Quilt (page 16) before you start this project.

WHAT YOU'LL NEED

- **Gold fabric:** 24½″ × 24½″ square
- **Backing:** 30″ × 30″
- **Batting:** 28″ × 28″
- **Binding:** 3 strips 2½″ × width of fabric
- **Scraps:** totaling about ½ yard, divided into lights and darks
- **Water-soluble fabric marker**

TECHNIQUES USED:

- Appliqué (page 17)
- Cutting (page 18)
- Piecing the Backing (page 28)
- Layering the Quilt Sandwich and Basting the Quilt (page 29)
- Quilting (page 31)
- Trimming and Binding the Quilt (page 42)

This fun little quilt uses the same sewing technique as the much larger Ticker Tape Quilt (page 104), a fast and fun way to make quilts. You sew through all three layers of the quilt to attach the small pieces, so the quilting is finished when you attach your last piece!

TIP: If you don't have a big collection of different fabrics, check out the remnant section of your local fabric store to find less expensive fabrics.

cutting

Colored fabrics:

Cut squares and rectangles of varying sizes, ranging from 2″ to 6″. Start with a pile of 20 pieces of light color and 10 pieces of dark color. You can cut more as you decide what color you want and how many you need.

Made by Angela Walters, using "ticker tape" technique
by Amanda Jean Nyberg

making the quilt

Use the Techniques Used list (page 66) to find more information if you need help.

Drawing the Heart

Using the water-soluble marker or a light pencil, draw a heart in the center of the gold fabric. Refer to the quilt photo for size: not too small and not too large. Don't worry if it's not perfect!

> *You could also try all kinds of shapes: a school logo, a simple shape such as a circle or triangle, or even your initial.*

Cloe

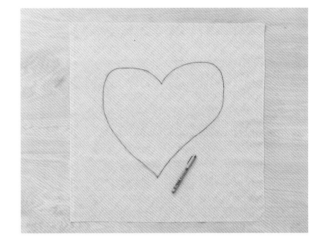

Layering and Basting

1. Make a quilt sandwich with the backing, batting, and gold fabric.

2. Baste the quilt sandwich.

Sewing on the Pieces

1. Starting at the center, place a piece of dark fabric on top of the quilt sandwich. Carefully sew the fabric onto the quilt sandwich about ¼″ away from the edge all the way around the piece of fabric. This stitching, which is called *raw-edge appliqué*, will serve as the quilting, too.

2. Continue sewing the scraps onto the quilt sandwich, leaving an inch or so between the pieces.

3. Use the darker fabrics inside the drawn heart and the lighter fabrics outside.

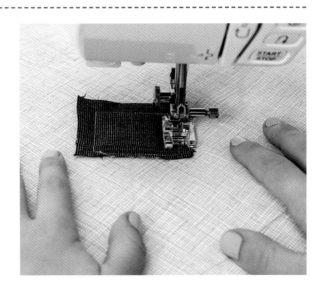

4. Fill in as completely as possible. Trim the scraps as needed to fit them in a certain space.

note

We cut a piece of dark fabric into a small triangle to form the bottom point of the heart.

Finishing

1. Carefully trim away the extra batting and backing.

2. Bind the quilt.

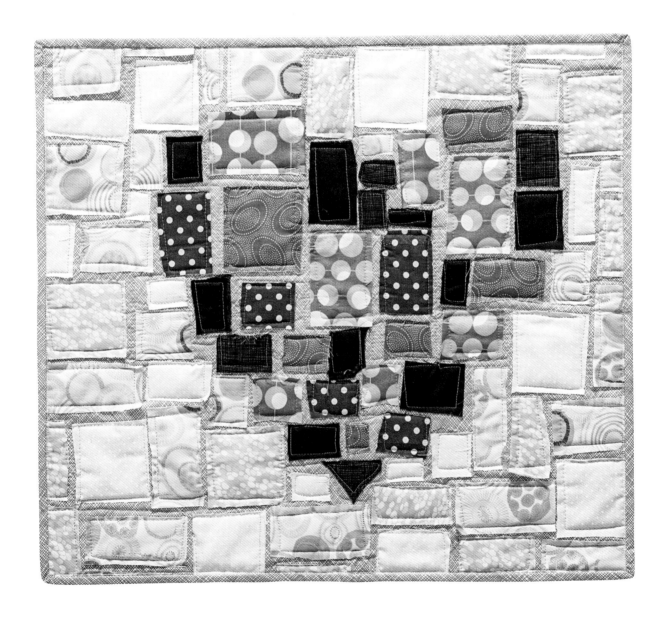

Tips and Ideas

Get a little fussy

To help your ticker tape show off your favorite fabrics, try *fussy cutting*. Fussy cutting involves cutting the fabric to get exactly the part you want, rather than just cutting strips or squares.

Make it scrappy

Throw all your scraps in a pile and use whichever one you grab. Scrappy-looking quilts can be so much fun.

See full project instructions for Ticker Tape Quilt (page 104).

Change the shape

Most ticker tape quilts are made with square or rectangular scraps of fabric, but you can be adventurous. Try different shapes such as triangles, circles, ovals, or any shape you like. This one uses a leaf-like shape with echo quilting inside the leaves.

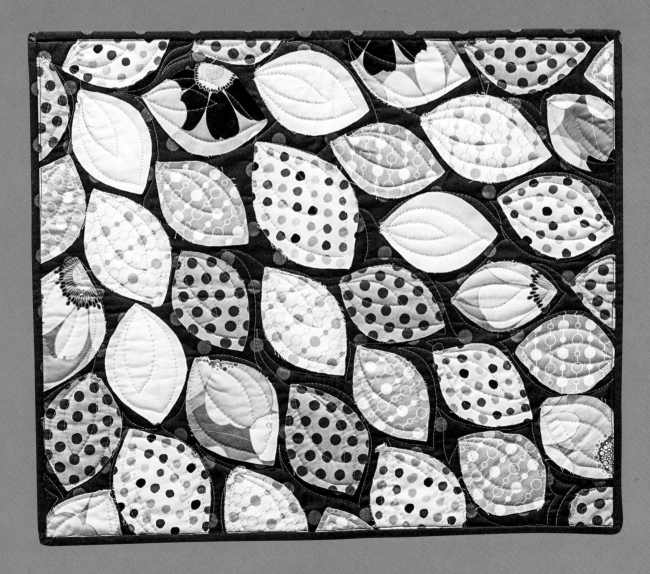

SKILL LEVEL 2

charmed quilt

Read Making a Quilt (page 16) before you start this project.

WHAT YOU'LL NEED

- **Charm packs:** total of 132 charms, or 5″ squares cut from various fabrics totaling 2½ yards

- **Backing:** 3 yards

- **Batting:** 54″ × 62″ piece, or twin-size package

- **Yarn or embroidery thread**

- **Needles**

- **Binding:** ½ yard

TECHNIQUES USED:

- Pressing (page 24)
- Sewing (page 24)
- Making the Quilt Top (page 26)
- Piecing the Backing (page 28)
- Layering the Quilt Sandwich and Basting the Quilt (page 29)
- Tie Quilting (page 36)
- Trimming and Binding the Quilt (page 42)

This quilt uses charm packs to let you get right to the fun part: sewing! You can experiment with finding the perfect look for your quilt as you develop skills in quilt construction, like ¼″ piecing and pressing of blocks and rows.

What Are Charm Packs?

A charm pack is a prepackaged bundle of squares already cut and ready to go. That means you can jump right into the sewing! A charm pack will often have designs from a fabric collection, so you

know the fabrics will look good together. Traditional charm quilts have blocks in which every single fabric is different, but charm packs usually contain two of each "charm." The most common size is 5″ × 5″, but 4″ × 4″ is also used, so check the size. The number of squares varies, so read the packaging to see how many charm packs you need.

If you can't find the perfect charm pack for your quilt, you can cut your own 5″ squares of your favorite fabrics.

Cloe chose these designs from the Fox Field collection by Tula Pink, and cut them into 5″ squares.

cutting

Cut 5 strips 2¼″ × width of fabric for the binding.

making the quilt

Use the Techniques Used list (page 72) to find more information if you need help.

Making the Quilt Top

Lay out the charm squares.

This is where you set your inner artist free. Arrange the squares in 11 rows with 12 blocks in each row. Put them in the order that you like. Move them around until you find the arrangement that looks best to you.

Using a Design Wall

A design wall is an area where you can lay out your blocks and view them as though they were sewn together. This makes it easy to find the perfect arrangement for your quilt. Making a design wall is so easy! All you need is a large piece of batting or a flannel-backed tablecloth. Tape it to a large wall and it's done. (Check with an adult to make sure it's okay!) Since the fabric squares cling to the flannel, you can easily move your blocks around until you find the exact arrangement you want.

If you don't have the space for a design wall or just don't feel like doing it, no problem; just lay the blocks on the floor.

Once you have decided on the layout, it's time to make the quilt top.

" When I can't decide, I use a digital camera or a phone camera to take a picture of each layout. It makes it easier to decide on the perfect one. "

Cloe

note

In this quilt, we combined precut charm packs with 5″ blocks that we cut ourselves. If you do this too, you will notice there may be a difference in size. Make sure to line up the blocks as shown.

Check size of charm squares.

Line up straight edge with inner points of pinked edge.

1. To make the quilt top, first sew the blocks into rows. To make it easier, you can try chain piecing.

2. Press all the seams in the first row going in the same direction. Press seams in the second row in the opposite direction, and alternate the pressing direction for each row.

3. Once all the rows are made, sew the rows together. The intersections will nest nicely because of the way you pressed the seams.

note _____

If you want to sew blocks together faster, try chain piecing. *Chain piecing* is sewing pairs of blocks together without cutting the thread in between.

It saves time and thread!

Layering, Basting, and Quilting

Piece the backing. Using the backing and batting, prepare a quilt sandwich.

You can quilt your charm quilt any way you would like, but Cloe decided to quilt hers by tying it.

Finishing

Trim and bind the quilt; show it off to all your friends.

rag quilt

Read Making a Quilt (page 16) before you start this project.

TECHNIQUES USED:

- Cutting (page 18)
- Sewing (page 24)
- Layering the Quilt Sandwich and Basting the Quilt (page 29)
- Machine Quilting (page 38)

If you want to make a super soft quilt, this flannel quilt is for you. The frayed edges of the quilt blocks add to the cuddly look. Each block is quilted before the quilt is put together. This means you can get to the best part faster: using the quilt.

cutting

Purple print:
Cut 21 strips 5″ × width of fabric; subcut into 168 squares 5″ × 5″.

Coordinating flannels:
Cut 6 strips 5″ × width of fabric from each of 4 fabrics; subcut into 42 squares 5″ × 5″ (total of 168 squares from all 4 coordinating flannels).

Batting:
Cut 168 squares 4″ × 4″.

making the quilt

Use the Techniques Used list (at left) to find more information if you need help.

Making the Square Units

1. For each unit, use 2 squares of the same color. Place 1 colored square wrong side up, center the batting on the colored square, and then place the

other colored square right side up on top, aligned exactly with the first colored square. Pin.

2. Mark a diagonal line from corner to corner using a water-soluble marker and ruler. If you prefer, you could just eyeball it. Sew on the diagonal. If you have a walking foot for your machine, you can use it to make the piecing easier.

3. Repeat Step 2 for the other diagonal to form an "X" on the block.

Don't worry if your "X" isn't perfect. These stitches serve as the quilting, so they will hold the layers together just fine.

4. Repeat Steps 1–3 to make quilted units out of all the 5˝ colored flannel squares. Make sure to use the same color on the front and back of each block.

TIP: If your machine has decorative stitches, you can use a different stitch for a fun look. Refer to your sewing machine's instruction manual to learn how to change the stitch.

Sewing the Units Together to Make the Blocks

1. Lay out 2 purple print blocks and 2 random-color blocks, as shown.

2. Sew the 2 purple print units along one edge using a ½˝ seam.

½˝
seam

3. Do the same with the other 2 squares.

4. Sew the 2 pairs together to make the block. Open the seams as you sew across the intersections (don't press to one side). Make sure the previously sewn seams are facing out.

5. Repeat Steps 1–4 until you have a total of 42 blocks.

note _____

The side of the finished block with the seam showing is the top side of the block.

Putting the Quilt Together

1. Arrange the blocks in rows.

2. Sew the blocks together in rows.

3. Then sew the rows together to make the quilt top.

4. Sew around the quilt ½˝ from the edge.

Finishing

1. Use scissors to carefully make small cuts into each seam. These cuts help create the fluffy texture along the seams. Be careful not to cut into the sewing lines!

2. Wash the quilt and enjoy the frayed goodness.

make it different

If you want to make your own pattern, you can arrange the blocks in the order you want. The plaid flannels in this quilt are laid out in a regular diagonal pattern.

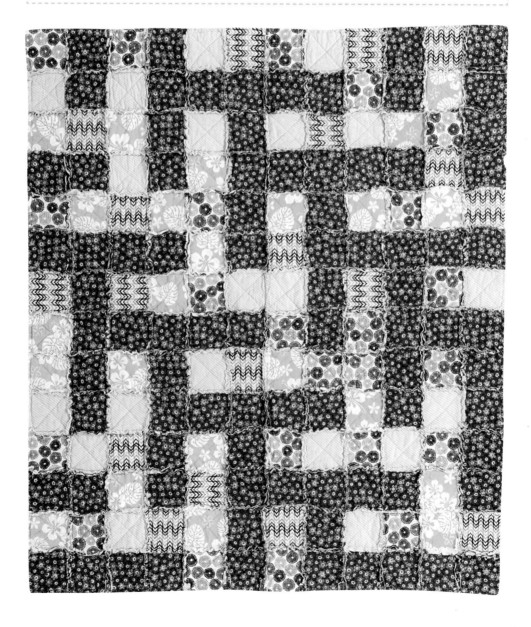

appliqué letter pillow

Read Making a Quilt (page 16) before you start this project.

WHAT YOU'LL NEED

Fabric for pillow front: ¼ yard each of 3 fabrics

> **TIP:** You can use scraps if they are at least 2½″ × 18½″.

Appliqué: 9″ × 9″ for the letter

Pillow top backing: 20″ × 20″ muslin or white lightweight fabric

Batting: 20″ × 20″

Hand-quilting thread

Pillow back: ⅜ yard fabric

Pillow form: 18″ × 18″

Paper-backed fusible adhesive: 9″ × 9″ (I use HeatnBond Lite.)

note

For this project, you'll need a pillow form, sold in craft stores and online. Pillow forms are available in different sizes and firmness levels. You will need one that is 18″ square.

TECHNIQUES USED:

Appliqué (page 17)

Cutting (page 18)

Pressing (page 24)

Sewing (page 24)

Layering the Quilt Sandwich and Basting the Quilt (page 29)

Quilting (page 31)

Trimming and Binding the Quilt (page 42)

The front of the Appliqué Letter Pillow is really a mini-quilt, which makes it perfect for practicing hand quilting. The design also uses a technique called appliqué to add a large initial monogram to the pillow. Cloe chose one of the easiest methods for appliqué. It's called raw-edge fusible appliqué, and it's fast and simple.

cutting

Colored fabrics:

Cut 3 strips 2½˝ × 18½˝ from each fabric.

Pillow back:

Cut 2 rectangles 11½˝ × 18½˝.*

* Refer to Cutting Wide Strips, Squares, and Rectangles (page 23) for help.

making the pillow

Use the Techniques Used list (page 84) to find more information if you need help.

Making the Pillow Top

1. Lay out the strips, alternating the fabrics.

2. Sew the strips together and press flat.

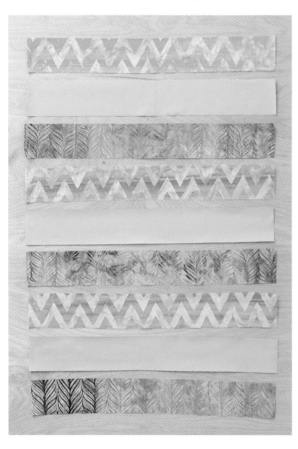

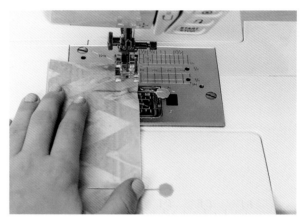

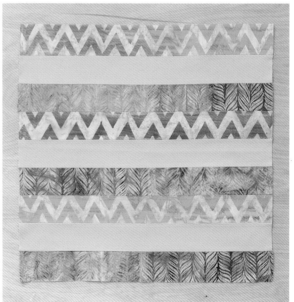

Adding Your Initial Using Fusible Appliqué --------------------------

Customize your pillow by adding your initial.

1. Read and follow the directions that came with your paper-backed fusible adhesive. They may be different from the instructions below.

2. Place the fusible adhesive, paper side on top, on the back (wrong side) of the fabric for the letter and smooth it with your hands.

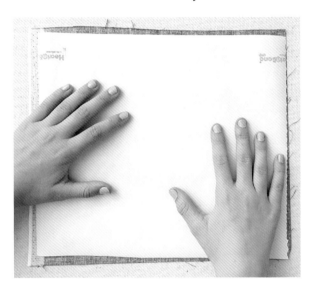

3. Press to melt the adhesive onto the fabric.

4. Turn it over and use a marking pencil to lightly draw a letter on top of the fabric. You can hand draw it or print out a letter from the computer to trace.

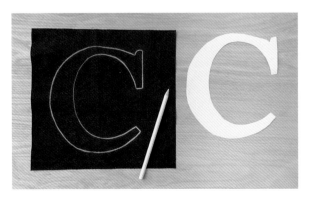

5. Cut out the letter using scissors, and peel off the paper.

6. Place the letter in the center of the pillow. Use a hot iron to melt the adhesive.

Layering, Basting, and Quilting

1. Using the pillow top, batting, and backing, prepare a quilt sandwich.

2. Hand quilt the pillow with straight lines. Cloe also outline quilted her appliqué to give it a custom look.

note

Even though we hand quilted our pillow, you can use any of the quilting techniques.

Finishing the Pillow

Now it's time to turn it into a pillow.

1. Trim away the excess backing and batting.

2. On both backing rectangles, press under ¼″ along an 18½″ side. Press under ¼″ again, and sew in place.

3. Lay the pillow top right side up. Place the backing rectangles on top, with the wrong side facing up and the finished edges toward the middle, and pin in place. The backing rectangles should overlap by about 3″.

4. Sew all the way around the pillow with a ¼″ seam.

5. Turn the pillow right side out, and gently poke the corners out so they are nice and square.

6. Insert the pillow form and put it in just the right spot on your bed!

change it up!

Instead of adding an initial to your pillow, you could use any kind of shape. In this variation, we decided to cut a flower shape.

Try playing around with the pillow and finding your favorite shape!

bed runner

Read Making a Quilt (page 16) before you start this project.

A bed runner is an easy way to customize your room. Make one using your favorite colors to add a "pop" of fun to your bed. This quick project will teach you how to make a half-square triangle, a simple but very useful quilting block. It might even make you want to make your bed.

cutting

Dark green print:
Cut 4 strips 7″ × width of fabric; subcut into 18 squares 7″ × 7″.

Cut 1 strip 6½″ × width of fabric; subcut into 4 squares 6½″ × 6½″.

Cut 1 piece 24½″ × width of fabric; subcut into 2 rectangles 20½″ × 24½″.*

Yellow print:
Cut 4 strips 7″ × width of fabric; subcut into 18 squares 7″ × 7″.

Binding:
Cut 7 strips 2¼″ × width of fabric.

Refer to Cutting Wide Strips, Squares, and Rectangles (page 23) for help.

making the bed runner

Use the Techniques Used list (page 90) to find more information if you need help.

Making the Blocks

1. Draw a diagonal line from a corner to the opposite corner of a yellow print 7″ × 7″ square.

2. Place a dark green square and a yellow square right sides together. Sew ¼″ on each side of the drawn line.

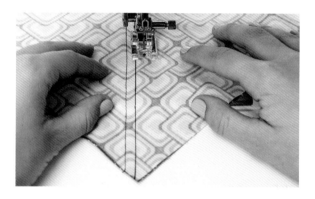

3. Using scissors or a rotary cutter, cut on the line.

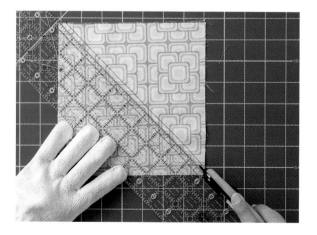

4. Carefully press the half-square triangles open.

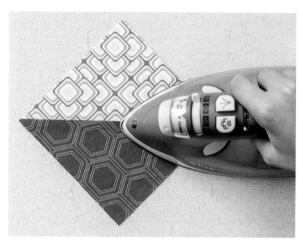

The result is 2 half-square triangle blocks.

5. Repeat Steps 1–4 for the rest of the 7″ squares. You should have 36 half-square triangles.

6. Check the size of each half-square triangle block. They should measure 6½″ square, but they may be oversized. Trim blocks to 6½″ square, if needed.

Assembling the Bed Runner

1. Using the diagram as a guide, lay out the half-square triangles and 4 squares 6½″ × 6½″ as shown.

2. Sew the blocks together to make the center of the runner.

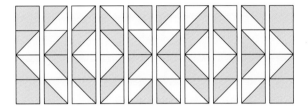

3. Sew the 20½″ × 24½″ rectangles to the sides of the center of the runner.

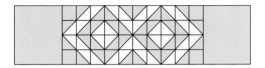

Layering, Basting, and Quilting

1. Piece the backing. Using the backing and batting, prepare a quilt sandwich.

2. Cloe and I decided this runner was perfect for straight-line machine quilting. To break it up a little bit, we alternated between straight lines and loopy lines. Of course, you can quilt the runner any way that you want.

Straight-line quilting, viewed from the front and back

Finishing

Carefully trim away the extra batting and backing, and bind.

scrappy variation

For a fun variation, you could make a scrappy version of the bed runner. Use random fabrics in similar colors for the half-square triangle blocks. The result is a runner that looks totally different!

SKILL LEVEL 2

cut-away rug

Read Making a Quilt (page 16) before you start this project.

WHAT YOU'LL NEED

- **Fabric A:** 1 yard for the top
- **Fabric B:** 1 yard for the fabric revealed under the top
- **Binding:** ⅓ yard
- **Backing:** 40″ × 44″
- **Batting:** 40″ × 44″ or a crib-size package
- **Sharp-pointed scissors**

TIPS: PICKING OUT FABRICS

For the project sample, Cloe and I decided to use linen for the top piece of fabric. It is a little more durable than cotton, so it will stand up to repeated use. It also has a really nice texture when quilted. We used a contrasting print for the second layer, which was revealed when we cut the linen.

TECHNIQUES USED:

- Cutting (page 18)
- Layering the Quilt Sandwich and Basting the Quilt (page 29)
- Quilting (page 31)
- Trimming and Binding the Quilt (page 42)

Time for free-motion quilting fun! This project is all about the quilting—no piecing is required. The Cut-Away Rug is perfect for personalizing your room or bathroom.

Fabrics A and B:
Cut each fabric to 36″ × 40½″.*

Binding:
Cut 4 strips 2¼″ × width of fabric.*

* Refer to Cutting Wide Strips, Squares, and Rectangles (page 23) for help.

FINISHED SIZE:
35½˝ × 40˝

making the rug

Use the Techniques Used list (page 94) to find more information if you need help.

Layering and Basting

1. Prepare the quilt sandwich with the backing, batting, fabric B, and then fabric A on top.

2. Baste the rug.

note

If you use basting spray to baste your quilts, make sure you don't use it between the top two fabrics of this project.

Quilting

Using a free-motion quilting foot, have fun quilting your favorite designs. Quilt all the layers together with as much quilting as you would like. See Free-Motion Machine Quilting (page 40) for quilting tips. Remember, try to think of it as "doodling" with thread.

Revealing the Design

When you are done quilting, the real fun begins. It's time to show the fun fabric underneath.

Using sharp-pointed scissors, carefully cut away only the *top fabric* between some of the quilted lines. Try not to cut the second layer of fabric underneath.

Finishing

1. Trim the rug and bind.

2. Wash it to give it a scrunchy, frayed vintage look.

All that's left to do is decide where to use your cool rug!

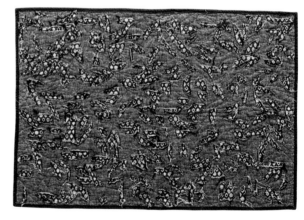

a different look

You can use a solid fabric on top, as we did. Or you can switch it up and put a cool printed fabric on top for a rug that really brightens up the room.

signature quilt

Read Making a Quilt (page 16) before you start this project.

WHAT YOU'LL NEED

- **Light blue solid:** 2⅛ yards

- **Coordinating prints:** scraps, totaling about 1 yard

- **Backing:** 1½ yards (usable fabric width of 44″)

- **Binding:** ⅜ yard

- **Batting:** 44″ × 54″

- **Color-safe fabric pens for signing blocks**

TECHNIQUES USED:

- Cutting (page 18)

- Pressing (page 24)

- Sewing (page 24)

- Layering the Quilt Sandwich and Basting the Quilt (page 29)

- Quilting (page 31)

- Trimming and Binding the Quilt (page 42)

Getting your friends' signatures isn't only for school yearbooks. Now you can always keep your friends' names and messages close with a Signature Quilt. You can ask your family, friends, or even teammates to celebrate your friendship by participating in your quilt.

cutting

Light blue solid:
Cut 9 strips 7½″ × width of fabric; subcut into 42 squares 7½″ × 7½″.*

Prints:
Cut 84 squares 3½″ × 3½″.

Binding:
Cut 5 strips 2¼″ × width of fabric.

* Refer to Cutting Wide Strips, Squares, and Rectangles (page 23) for help.

making the quilt

Use the Techniques Used list (page 98) to find more information if you need help.

Making the Blocks

1. On the back of each of the 3½˝ squares, draw a diagonal line from a corner to the opposite corner.

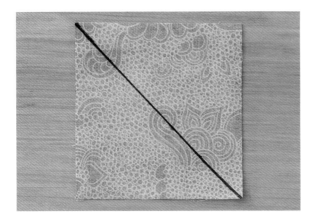

2. Choose 2 of the 3½˝ squares and place them face down on a light blue square, positioned as shown.

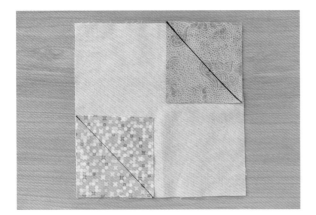

3. Sew on the lines. Trim off the corners by cutting ¼˝ away from the sewn line. Press open toward the triangle.

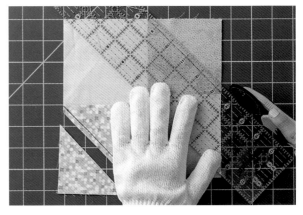

4. Use a 3½˝ square of a different fabric and repeat Steps 1–3 on the opposite corner of the block.

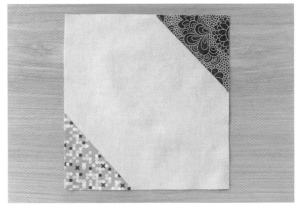

Signing the Blocks

This is the best time to have your friends sign the blocks, since you can easily pass them around before sewing them together.

■ **Get the right kind of pen.**

You may want to reach for your favorite glittery pen or Sharpie marker, but those aren't the best pens for fabric. Since the blocks will be in a quilt, you want to choose an ink that will stand up to washing and use. My favorite pen for signature quilts is the Pigma pen.

No matter which pen you choose, try it out first. Sign a test block and let the ink dry for 24 hours. Throw the block in the washer and see if it fades. It may take a little longer, but testing can save you a lot of trouble in the long run!

■ **Sign it right.**

When you pass the blocks out to your friends, make sure you tell them to stay away from the edges of the block. You would hate to cut off a friend's name in the seam allowance when you sew the blocks together.

■ **Encourage them to get creative.**

Why stick to just a plain ol' name? Encourage your friends to draw funny pictures, write a note, or color in their names. These blocks have plenty of room, so let their creativity shine!

■ **Set the ink.**

Read the instructions on the pens to see if heat setting is needed to make the ink permanent. If so, go ahead and set the ink now, following the instructions.

Assembling the Quilt

Once you get all of your signed blocks back, it's time to put them together into a very special quilt!

1. Arrange the blocks in rows.

2. Sew the blocks together in rows.

3. Then sew the rows together.

Layering, Basting, and Quilting

1. Using the backing and batting, prepare a quilt sandwich.

2. Quilt your signature quilt any way that you like. With this quilt, Cloe wanted to machine quilt using the walking foot on her sewing machine. She used the diagonal lines of the block as a guide for the quilting.

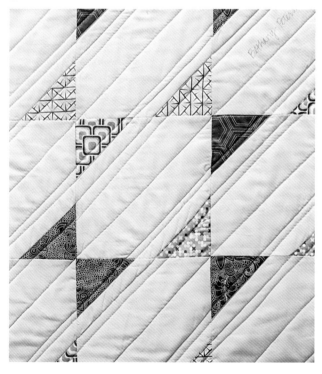

Finishing

Carefully trim away the extra batting and backing, and bind the quilt.

Be sure to show off the finished quilt to all your friends who signed the blocks.

ticker tape quilt

Read Making a Quilt (page 16) before you start this project.

WHAT YOU'LL NEED

- **White fabric:** 3⅝ yards
- **Backing:** 4 yards
- **Batting:** 68″ × 84″ piece
- **Scraps:** totaling about 3 yards
- **Binding:** ⅔ yard

> **TIP:** If you don't have a big collection of different fabrics, check out the remnant section of your local fabric store to find less expensive fabrics.

TECHNIQUES USED:

- Appliqué (page 17)
- Cutting (page 18)
- Piecing the Backing (page 28)
- Layering the Quilt Sandwich and Basting the Quilt (page 29)
- Quilting (page 31)
- Trimming and Binding the Quilt (page 42)

What do you do when you have a bunch of small scraps of fabric? You make a colorful, scrappy Ticker Tape Quilt. This quilt technique was developed by Amanda Jean Nyberg and is a fast and fun way to make quilts. The best thing about this technique is that you are quilting it as you go. We gave this quilt a skill level of 3 because of its large size; the sewing technique is easy. For a smaller quilt that uses this appliqué technique, see the Heart Ticker Tape Quilt (page 66).

note

This quilt is customizable! You don't have to make your Ticker Tape Quilt as large as I did. Try making it smaller if you are still trying to get the hang of quilting. Just make the quilt sandwich the size you want the quilt to be.

cutting

Colored fabrics:
Cut squares and rectangles of varying sizes, ranging from 2″ to 6″. Start with a stack of 70 shapes, and cut more as you need them to fill the whole area. More than 400 squares and rectangles are in our quilt.

Binding:
Cut 8 strips 2¼″ × width of fabric.

FINISHED SIZE:
Approximately
61½″ × 77½″
(This is huge!)

making the quilt

Use the Techniques Used list (page 104) to find more information if you need help.

Layering and Basting

1. Cut the white fabric into 2 pieces 1¾ yards each.

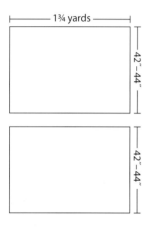

2. Sew them together along the longer edge. Trim about 5″ off the bottom so you have a piece that measures 62″ × 78″.

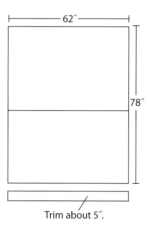

3. Repeat Steps 1 and 2 for the backing fabric, cutting each piece 68″ long and not trimming after sewing the pieces together.

4. Make a quilt sandwich with the white fabric, batting, and backing.

5. Baste the quilt sandwich.

Sewing On the Pieces

1. Starting in the center of the quilt, place a piece of fabric on top of the quilt sandwich. Carefully sew the fabric onto the quilt about ¼″ away from the edges all the way around the piece of fabric. This stitching serves as the quilting, too.

2. Keep sewing on scraps, leaving an inch or so between the pieces.

3. Fill in as completely as possible. Trim scraps if you need to fit them in a certain space.

TIP: Pivot with the needle down when you need to turn at each corner. Make sure the backing and batting don't get bunched up as you get ready to sew the next side of each square or rectangle.

Finishing

1. Carefully trim away the extra batting and backing.

2. Bind the quilt.

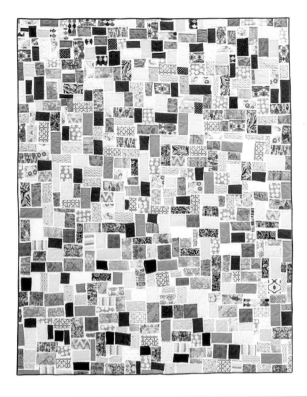

More Ideas for Ticker Tape Quilts

There are lots of things you can do with Ticker Tape quilts. Here are some more ideas. — Cloe

Try a regular layout

Instead of a random, scrappy layout of the quilt, try laying out the fabric pieces in a regulated order. Trim the pieces to fit.

Make a design

After you baste the quilt sandwich, use a water-soluble marker to lightly draw a large shape on the quilt top. Almost any large shape will work: a heart, your school logo, or a letter.

Use one fabric color inside the shape and another outside the shape to make the shape appear clearly.

Get your friends involved

If you have friends who like to make quilts, you can make a party out of it! Trade fabric pieces with them or have them sign some of the scraps before you get started.

SKILL LEVEL 3

school supply roll

Read Making a Quilt (page 16) before you start this project.

TECHNIQUES USED:

- Cutting (page 18)
- Pressing (page 24)
- Sewing (page 24)
- Layering the Quilt Sandwich and Basting the Quilt (page 29)
- Quilting (page 31)
- Trimming and Binding the Quilt (page 42)

You won't mind going to school when you can carry your school supplies in style. This project is perfect for learning machine quilting as well as practicing basic sewing.

cutting

Fabric A:

Cut 1 rectangle 6½″ × 18″.*

Cut 1 rectangle 11″ × 21″.*

Fabric B:

Cut 1 strip 2½″ × 18″.

Cut 1 rectangle 6″ × 18″.

Cut 1 strip 3½″ × 24″.

* Refer to Cutting Wide Strips, Squares, and Rectangles (page 23) for help.

making the school supply roll

Use the Techniques Used list (page 108) to find more information if you need help.

Making the Roll

1. Sew the 6½″ × 18″ rectangle of fabric A to the 2½″ × 18″ strip of fabric B.

2. Make a quilt sandwich out of the block. Use the batting in the middle and the 11″ × 21″ rectangle of fabric A as the back. (The "back" will be the interior of the school supply roll.)

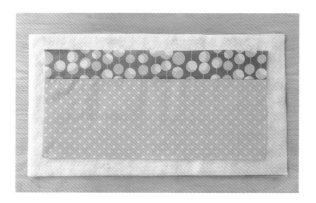

3. Quilt the layers together. Trim away the extra backing and batting.

For this project, we quilted horizontal lines and along the top and bottom edges.

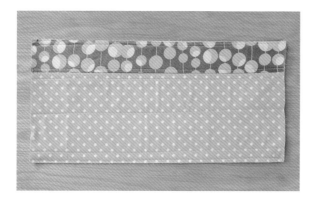

4. Press under ¼″ along 1 long side of the 6″ × 18″ rectangle of fabric B.

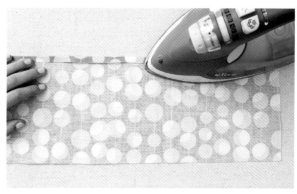

5. Sew along the fold to hold it in place. This is the top edge of the pocket section.

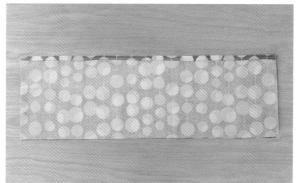

6. Place the quilted section from Step 3 with the pieced side facing down. Place the fabric B rectangle on top, right side up. Line up the sides and bottom of the fabric B rectangle with the quilted piece, and pin in place.

7. Divide the supply roll into 3 parts by sewing 2 lines from top to bottom.

8. To make dividers to hold your pencils and pens, stitch lines about 1″ apart.

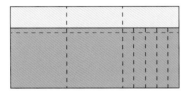

You can vary the spacing if you want some dividers to hold smaller items.

9. Sew ¼″ from the edge, leaving 2″ open at the center of the left side, where the strap will go.

Making and Adding the Strap

1. Fold the 3½″ × 24″ strip of fabric B in half, wrong sides together, and press to make a crease.

2. Open the strip, and fold each side to meet at the center crease. Press.

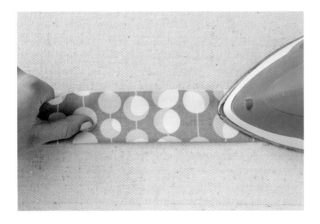

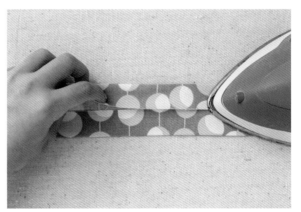

3. Fold it in half again, so the strap is about ⅞″ wide.

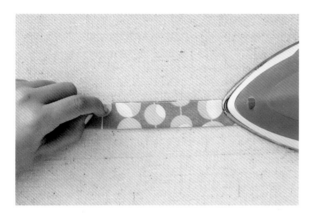

4. Sew the strap closed by sewing ¼″ from the folded edges.

5. Fold the strap in half. Place the folded edge of the strap into the opening, tucking about 1″ of the fold inside. Sew the opening ¼″ from the edge to attach the strap.

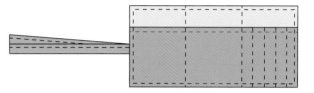

6. Use a zigzag stitch to sew all the way around the edge of the holder, securing the strap, too.

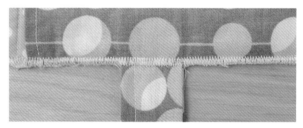

----- **TIP:** Refer to your sewing machine owner's manual to learn how to sew zigzag stitches. Experiment with stitch width and length to get the right spacing.

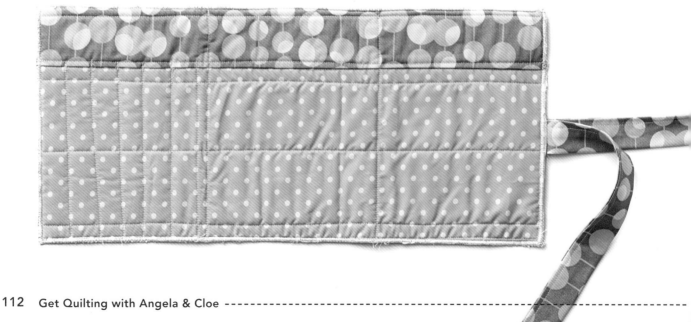

7. Fill with your pens and pencils. Fold in thirds and tie using the strap.

"The next time I make this, I am going to make one to match my water bottle holder."

Cloe

t-shirt quilt

Read Making a Quilt (page 16) before you start this project.

WHAT YOU'LL NEED

- **T-shirts:** 16
- **Backing:** 3¼ yards
- **Batting:** 58″ × 58″ piece, or a twin-size package
- **Binding:** ½ yard
- **Interfacing:** 6½ yards of 18″-wide lightweight iron-on interfacing
- **Template:** 13″ × 13″ piece of cardboard, poster board, or stiff paper
- **Pencil**

note _____

Most T-shirts are made of knit fabric. Knits are very stretchy and can be hard to work with. Iron-on interfacing adds stability to the T-shirt, making it easier to cut out. You can find interfacing sold by the yard at craft stores, usually 18″–20″ wide.

TECHNIQUES USED:

- Cutting (page 18)
- Pressing (page 24)
- Sewing (page 24)
- Making the Quilt Top (page 26)
- Piecing the Backing (page 28)
- Layering the Quilt Sandwich and Basting the Quilt (page 29)
- Quilting (page 31)
- Tie Quilting (page 36)
- Trimming and Binding the Quilt (page 42)

Do you have T-shirts you don't want to get rid of that you collected from teams, clubs, and groups? Don't just leave them in your drawer. Turn them into an extra warm quilt that will fill you with good memories.

cutting

Binding:
Cut 6 strips 2¼″ × width of fabric.

FINISHED SIZE:
50˝ × 50˝

making the t-shirt quilt

Use the Techniques Used list (page 114) to find more information if you need help.

Getting the Shirts Ready

1. Using scissors, roughly cut out the front or back of the shirt with the graphic you want to use in your quilt. It doesn't have to be perfect, since you will square it up later. Make sure the rough cut is large enough to cut out the 13″ × 13″ square later.

2. Place the cut T-shirt right side down on the ironing surface. Lay the interfacing, glue side down, on the T-shirt. Trim away any interfacing that hangs over the edge of the shirt.

> ----- **TIP:** Iron-on, or fusible, interfacing has an adhesive side and a smooth side. Generally, the adhesive side has a bumpy or slightly sticky feel. The bumps are small dots of glue that melt when heated by the iron. Make sure you place the adhesive side against the wrong side of the T-shirt.

3. Using an iron set on the temperature listed in the interfacing instructions, iron the interfacing to the T-shirt.

> ----- **TIP:** The hot iron might melt some graphics on the T-shirt. To prevent that, lay a piece of plain fabric under the graphic before ironing.

note

The 13″ square worked well for all of Cloe's T-shirts. If your T-shirts are much smaller or bigger, make the template smaller or bigger too. The most important thing is that all T-shirts be cut the same size, so your blocks can be the same size.

4. Place the cardboard template on top of the T-shirt, covering the graphic. Make sure the logo on the T-shirt is inside the template area. Use a pencil or fabric marker to trace around the edges of the cardboard.

5. Carefully cut on the lines using either a rotary cutter or scissors.

6. Repeat Steps 1–5 for the rest of the T-shirts.

TIP: Once the T-shirt blocks are cut, try not to handle them too much. The fusible might come unstuck.

Assembling the Quilt Top

1. Find an open space on the floor or a large table to lay out the quilt blocks. Arrange them into 4 rows with 4 T-shirts in each row, putting the shirts in the order you want.

TIP: Since you cut all the shirts to the same size, you can arrange them in any order! Try arranging them by color or from oldest to newest.

2. Place 2 T-shirt blocks right sides together and sew, using a ¼˝ seam allowance.

TIP: It will help to use your walking foot, if you have one, and sew slowly.

3. Continue to sew the blocks into rows, and then sew the rows together.

Layering, Basting, and Quilting

1. Piece the backing. Using the backing and batting, prepare a quilt sandwich.

2. This is a heavy quilt top because of the interfacing and T-shirt material. It might be difficult to machine quilt or even hand quilt. Tie quilting would be a good choice for this quilt.

Since my mom has a longarm quilting machine, she quilted it for me. If I were going to quilt it myself I would have definitely used tie quilting.

Cloe

make a coordinating pillow

If you have a leftover T-shirt, you can use it to make a pillow. It makes a fun addition to your quilt. Prepare the T-shirt with the interfacing just as you did for the quilt, and refer to Finishing the Pillow (page 88). You will need a 14˝ × 14˝ pillow form and 2 rectangles of fabric 8˝ × 13˝ for the pillow back.

Finishing

Trim and bind the quilt, and show it off to all your friends!

cuddle quilt

Read Making a Quilt (page 16) before you start this project.

There is nothing better than snuggling under a quilt, especially while watching a movie or cheering on your school's football team. Both the front and back of this soft, warm quilt are made of Cuddle, a plush, minky-style microfiber fabric. Working with Cuddle fabric is a little different from using the quilting cottons. It takes some special handling, but it's worth it. Cuddle comes 60˝ wide, making it wider than the usual quilting fabrics. It is thick and plush enough that we won't use a batting layer for this project. With just a little effort, you will have a quilt perfect for snuggling.

WHAT YOU'LL NEED

--- **Fabric A:** 1 yard

--- **Fabric B:** 1⅛ yards

--- **Fabric C:** ½ yard

--- **Backing:** 2 yards
(using 60˝-wide Cuddle)

TECHNIQUES USED:

--- Cutting (page 18)

--- Sewing (page 24)

--- Piecing the Backing (page 28)

--- Layering the Quilt Sandwich and Basting the Quilt (page 29)

--- Tie Quilting (page 36)

Using Cuddle Fabric

■ **It can be messy!**
When cutting the Cuddle fabric, the first thing you will notice is that it leaves little bits of fabric and fuzz behind. Using a rotary cutter will make less of a mess, but it's still a good idea to have a vacuum cleaner ready to clean up your mess when you're done.

■ **Get the pins ready.**
You will definitely need to use pins as you make this quilt. The edges of the Cuddle fabric tend to curl a bit and can stretch, so more pinning than usual is necessary to keep your pieces even and aligned.

■ **Double the seam allowance.**
Most quilt pattern instructions tell you to sew the blocks ¼˝ from the edge of the fabric (this distance is called the *seam allowance*). But this fabric will behave better if you double the seam allowance, so we will use a ½˝ seam allowance.

■ **Don't touch the iron!**
Most quilt pattern instructions tell you to press seams, but Cuddle is different. Do not press the seams of your Cuddle Quilt because the minky-style fabric can melt! In fact, do not press any part of the Cuddle Quilt at all. It doesn't need it. The fabric doesn't hold a wrinkle and you can smooth it out using your hands.

cutting

Fabric A:

Cut 2 strips 16″ × width of fabric; subcut each strip into 1 rectangle 16″ × 19″ and 1 rectangle 16″ × 35″. Trim 2″ off the long side of the 16″ × 35″ rectangles to make 2 rectangles 14″ × 35″ (for a total of 4 rectangles).*

Fabric B:

Cut 1 strip 22″ × width of fabric; subcut into 2 rectangles 22″ × 28″.*

Cut 1 strip 16″ × width of fabric; subcut into 2 rectangles 16″ × 17″.*

Fabric C:

Cut 2 strips 8″ × width of fabric; subcut each strip into 1 rectangle 8″ × 35″ and 1 rectangle 8″ × 22″ (total of 4 rectangles).*

Refer to Cutting Wide Strips, Squares, and Rectangles (page 23) for help.

----- TIPS: CUTTING CUDDLE

Since the Cuddle fabric is so wide and fuzzy, it can be a little harder to manage than cotton fabric. To help make it easier, try the following steps:

1. Fold the fabric twice to make cutting a little easier. Make sure the edges stay as straight as possible. Check fabric at the fold to make sure it is lined up smoothly.

2. Unfold the strip to cut into smaller pieces.

3. If your table isn't big enough to lay out the strip, you can lay it on the floor. Use a measuring tape and scissors to cut.

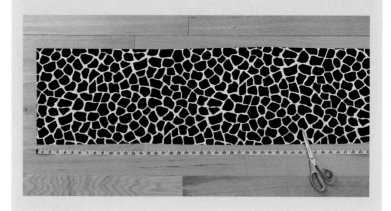

making the quilt

Use the Techniques Used list (page 120) to find more information if you need help.

Making the Blocks --

This quilt consists of two block designs: Block A and Block B.

BLOCK A

1. Pin the 16″ × 19″ rectangle of fabric A to the 16″ × 17″ rectangle of fabric B, pinning along the 16″ side. Place the pins about 1″ apart. Carefully sew together using a ½″ seam.

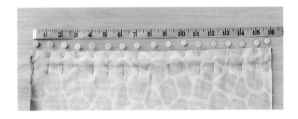

2. Sew the large side of the unit to the 35″ side of the 14″ × 35″ rectangle of fabric A.

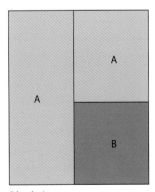

Block A

3. Make 2 blocks.

BLOCK B

1. Sew the 22″ × 28″ rectangle of fabric B to the 8″ × 22″ rectangle of fabric C, sewing along the 22″ side.

2. Sew the 8″ × 35″ rectangle of fabric C to the long side of the unit.

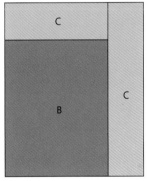

Block B

3. Make 2 blocks.

Assembling the Quilt

1. Sew Block A and Block B together as shown.

2. Sew the 2 sections together.

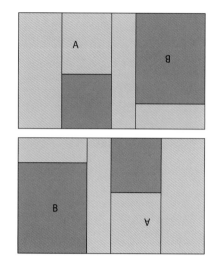

Finishing

How you decide to finish this project is up to you! You can machine quilt it just as you would a "regular" quilt. Or, since this fabric is thick and plush, you can leave it unquilted.

We used a different finishing technique for this project. Cloe and I will show you how to finish the edges using a technique called *pillowcasing*.

1. Piece the backing if needed. Lay the backing fabric face up on a large, flat surface, such as the floor.

2. Lay the pieced top of the Cuddle Quilt face down on top of the backing.

note _____

It's okay if the backing is larger than the top. You can trim it at the end.

3. Pin the 2 layers together using a pin every 1″–2″. Be sure both sides of the quilt stay as flat as possible.

4. Starting from the middle of one side of the quilt, sew a ½″ seam around the whole quilt, stopping about 6″ from the starting point.

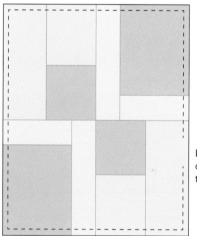

Leave 6″ open for turning.

note _____

Be sure to leave 6″ open. You will need that opening to turn the quilt right side out.

5. Reach inside where you left the 6″ opening, and turn the quilt right side out. Smooth out the quilt and make sure it lies flat, paying special attention to the corners.

6. Fold under the open edges and pin closed.

7. Sew around the finished edge with a ½″ seam, making sure you secure the pinned edges in your stitching. Quilting is not really necessary for the Cuddle Quilt, but you might want to add some for interest.

Sew ½″ from edge around all sides.

 I love my Cuddle Quilt, but I wanted to add a little more to it. So I decided to add some knots to my quilt using tie quilting. Of course, I used my favorite color thread, hot pink! **"**

Cloe

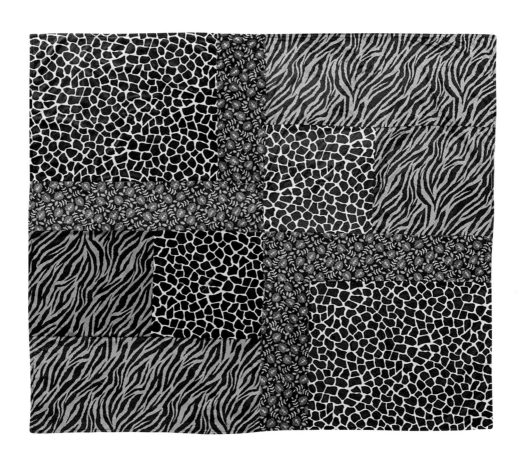

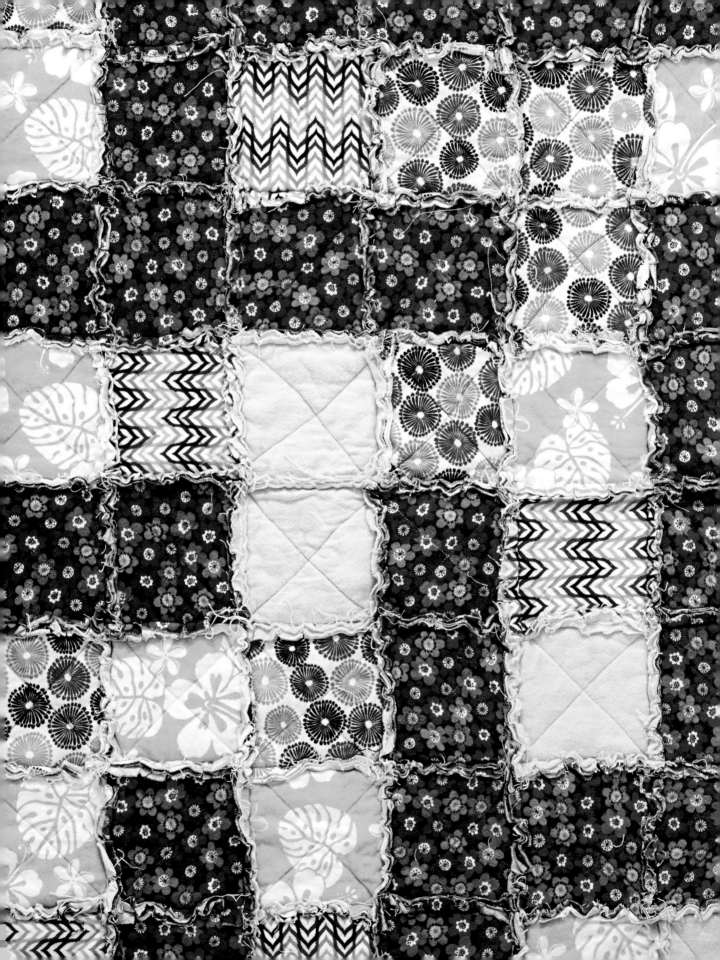

about the authors

Quilting is a family affair for Angela and Cloe Walters, a mother–daughter quilting duo. When she's not bugging her mom to use the longarm, Cloe can be found at the sewing machine or running around outside. Angela is a longarm quilter, author, and coffee addict who thinks quilting is the funnest part of making a quilt. Angela, Cloe, and the rest of their family live on the outskirts of Kansas City.

ANGELA AND CLOE

ALSO BY ANGELA WALTERS:

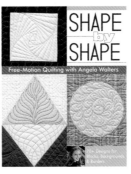

For more of Angela's tips and finished quilts, see her blog, Quilting Is My Therapy (quiltingismytherapy.com).

FunStitch
× × × × × × × × × ×
S T U D I O

stitch your art out.

FunStitch Studio books are written and designed specifically with kids, tweens, and teens in mind!

The text and projects are age appropriate and *nurture the love of handmade* in budding sewists, quilters, embroiderers, and fashion designers.

"Every time I finish a project, **I get so excited**, because I feel like I can do **anything!**"
— Annalise, age 12

by Ali Benyon

by Allison Nicoll

by Erin Hentzel

FunStitch
S T U D I O
an imprint of C&T Publishing